Liberty Loving Lion

Liberty Loving Lion

Unexpected Company of Lionel Durand

Morgan Zo Callahan & John F. Suggs

Dedicated by Morgan to:

Wife Dori, son David (Gravy), daughter-in-law Betty, grandson Morgan Jr., and granddaughter Penelope; Fay, Rosa, George, Evelyn, Maddie, David Li, Andy, Christine, Wayne, Joanne, Fabio Allen, Sophy, Jeanelle, Tim, Mama and Papa Fu; Compañeros y Compañeras,

Lionel Durand, my father; Vee, my mother; and Barbara, my sister - treasured all; Helen Callahan, Morgan Callahan Sr. and Mary Callahan, my cherished adopted parents and sister; nephews, Lionel Changeur and Jérémy Changeur; Celine and Richard; François Pierre-Louis Jr.

Simone Staco Rivière, my lovely cousin who graciously opened the door to Lionel Durand; Martine Rivière, Pascale Rivière, Marc-Adrien Rivière, Lucien Rivière, Eduard Gros, Sébastien Stark, Josiane Stark, Micheline Durand, Michel Durand, Olivier Durand, Chantal Laroche, and Christopher Freedom Laroche

Beloved friend and brother, accomplished Investigative Genetic Genealogist John F. Suggs; Esteemed scholar, Los Angeles Loyola High School loved classmate (1962) Robert R. Rahl

Rev. Michael Saso, friend, venerable brother, teaching Ignatian, Buddhist, and Taoist wisdom; Ken Ireland from San Francisco days to present-day connecting from Dharamsala and Bangkok

Nini and Gary, Joe and Kathy, John and Melinda, Sandy and Jennifer, William and Patricia Linda, Amy, Holly, Danny, Thuy, Kobe, Howie, Lon and Hahn

War-time correspondents, past and present, whose unique skills, bravery, and grace under pressure ensure that vital stories are told.

Dedicated by John to:

To my children, Rachel Lynn Suggs and John Joshua Devlin Suggs.

To all the members, past and present, of the Society of Jesus, you have been my friends, mentors, and beloved companions along the way.

To all the members of the Magdala Community whose abiding faith filled presence steadfastly nourishes and sustains me.

Honoring Lionel Durand

Born December 22, 1920
Port-au-Prince, Haiti

Died January 14, 1961
Paris, France

Morgan Zo Callahan

Morgan Zo Callahan lived ten life-transforming years as a Jesuit; he trained as a community organizer at the Saul Alinsky Institute in Chicago with John Baumann and Jerry Helfrich. For eighteen years, he taught mental fitness at convalescent hospitals and mental health community clinics, where he became involved in healing personal and collective trauma and in providing hospice support. Currently he teaches ESL part-time at El Monte-Rosemead Adult School in El Monte, California.

He's been fortunate to have traveled widely, meeting along the way many people with richly diverse cultures in Taiwan, South Korea, Mexico, El Salvador, Spain, Morocco, Costa Rica, Canada, Guatemala, Nicaragua, Honduras, Italy, the Bahamas, the Dominican Republic, and the USA.

Morgan is the author of *Notes of a Therapist: My View as a Special Education Teacher and Recreation Therapist*, published 1989; *Red Buddhist Envelope*, published 2010; *Bamboo Bending*, published 2014, edited by Sanford H. Perliss; *Revelation and Healing: A Father and Son Reunion*, published 2021; and the co-author (26 contributors) of *Intimate Meanderings: Conversations Close to Our Hearts,* published 2009 by iUniverse, edited by Ken Ireland.

He contributed a chapter to *Transitions in the Lives of Jesuits and Former Jesuits* and one to *A Thousand Hands: A Guidebook to Caring for Your Buddhist Community*, published by Sumeru Press. Morgan's magazine articles have appeared in *Karmakaze* and *Common Sense* (Los Angeles Buddhist Union).

His poetry has been published in anthologies of the Southern California Haiku Study Group: 2013 (*Dandelion Breeze*), 2014 (*Apology of Wild Flowers*), 2016 (*What the Wind Can't Touch*), 2017 *(Eclipse Moon)*, 2020 (*A Sonic Boom of Stars*) and 2023 (*Red Paper Parasols*); *American Poetry Anthology*, Volume VII, No. 5, 1988; *All My Tomorrows*, Volume VI, 1993; *Full Moon Poetry Society*, 2011 and 2012; *Street Sheet The 2017 Poetry Issue*; *Atlas Poetica: A Journey of Poetry of Place in Contemporary Tanka* (Summer2012); and the *Altadena Poetry Review Anthology* 2018.

Morgan edited *A Thousand Invisible Cords: An American Lawyer's Unorthodox Journey*, by Sanford H. Perliss, 2012 and *Geographic Recordings of the South China Sea Islands, An Historic 1946 Surveying Expedition to the South China Sea Islands* by Cheng Tsu-yueh, 2017.

John F. Suggs

As Founder and President of Family Orchard, LLC, John F. Suggs has over two decades of experience as an Investigative Genetic Genealogist specializing in analyzing DNA as well as in the more traditional research practices to assist Adult Adoptees search for and reunite with their birth parents and birth siblings.

A former Jesuit, John was trained in community organizing by Myles Horton of the Highlander Folk School, the same educator who heavily influenced Rosa Parks and Dr. Martin Luther King Jr. He also trained with John Baumann, S.J., Jerry Helfrich, S.J. and their team at PICO (now Faith in Action). Both organizations have impacted thousands of local community networks working both nationally and internationally.

John worked as a homeless advocate before becoming a founder and the first Executive Director of the Los Angeles Coalition to End Hunger and Homelessness. In that capacity, he developed and implemented numerous grassroots political and media campaigns targeting changes in public policies. He was a key player in organizing a homeless class action lawsuit against the County of Los Angeles in response to their draconian homeless policies, and successfully negotiated a $36 million dollar settlement. He also co-convened, in 1990, the very first conference in the nation on educating homeless children.

John served as Outreach Director and Fundraiser for the film *RFK in the Land of Apartheid: A Ripple of Hope.* The film documented a little known, yet important visit by Senator Robert F. Kennedy to South Africa in June 1966. John wrote the film's Teacher's Study Guide whose lessons included the vital role that engagement and dialogue play in responding to difficult and destructive public policies, and examples of ordinary people who found ways to stand up to an unjust system.

As a lead investigator for the Los Angeles City Ethics Commission, John successfully conducted a series of investigations into bribes to elected officials, resulting in the largest governmental ethics financial settlement in US History.

In partnership with the University of California, Los Angeles (UCLA) School of Public Health and the Los Angeles County Department of Health Services, John served as founding Executive Director for the Institute for Community Leadership, a nonprofit training and educational program that focused on developing and strengthening leadership skills within the public and nonprofit sectors.

John served five two-year terms in local office as an elected member of his Town's Council.

He holds a BA in Political Science from Loyola Marymount University, an MS in Management and Systems from New York University and an MBA from Fordham University.

Table of Contents

Acknowledgements

Preface

ACKNOWLEDGMENTS

Thanks to Professor Bill Chen and his associates at the University of the West for skillfully and patiently helping us create the initial shared platform for this book.

Heart-felt gratitude to Morgan's cousins, Micheline Durand and Michel Durand, for welcoming him warmly as a member of the Durand family, sharing with us revealing stories about their Uncle Lionel, whom they knew and greatly esteemed, and for providing the photos of Louis Durand and Madeleine de Pradines, Lionel's father and mother.

Warm appreciation for Morgan's Haitian cousins who all shared information with us so generously and willingly about Lionel and the extended family: Simone Staco Rivière, Chantal Laroche, Chris Freedom Larouche, Martine Rivière and Eduard Gross, Pascale Rivière, Marc-Adrien Rivière, Olivier Durand, Sébastien Stark, Josiane Stark.

Merci beaucoup to Lionel Changeur and Jérémy Changeur, Morgan's nephews, for helping us to know their grandfather Lionel better, as well as their grandmother Irène and beloved mother, Barbara. Lionel and Jérémy kindly provided us with family photos along with the remarkable Jean Cocteau and Pablo Picasso images which appear in this book.

Fond admiration for our Writing Companions: Robert R. Rahl, Don Maloney and Jeremy Rahl (who created a highly praised artistic cover, using Lionel Durand's portrait of his daughter, Barbara, as the front cover of our earlier book, 'Revelation and

Healing: *A Father and Son Reunion '*). We are forever indebted to Don Maloney and Robert R. Rahl, our dear friends and brothers, for their ongoing support, encouragement, and feedback.

To Professor Robert Gildea, University of Oxford, for his clarifying research on the French Resistance and to his colleague, Ludivine Broch, University of Westminster, for her paper, "Colonial Subjects and Citizens in the French Internal Resistance, 1940-1944," which gives an account of underappreciated non-white members of the French Resistance.

Our thanks go out to Rachel Suggs, John's daughter, who made several in-person attempts in Paris to obtain Lionel's and young Barbara's letters to Pablo Picasso which continue to reside uncategorized and unavailable until a later date in the Picasso Museum and Foundation, Musée Picasso-Paris.

Grazie, dear readers for your kind interest in our story of Lionel Durand.

PREFACE

*"I live my life in widening circles that reach out across
the world. I may not complete the last one, but I give
myself to it."*
Rainer Maria Rilke

*"He knew Paris as well as he knew the keyboard of his
battered typewriter; he brought it alive in his cables.*
Newsweek January 23, 1961

Lionel at Work

1961 Loyola Los Angeles High School Yearbook Production Staff
L to R: Schoolmates around their typewriter, S. Wood, D. Ucker, L. Lee (sitting), C. Solis, R. Rahl,
M. Callahan, B. Russell (editor), J. Ripple

> *"When it comes to racism, discrimination, corruption, public lies, dictatorships, and human rights, you have to take a stand as a reporter because I think our responsibility as a journalist is to confront those who are abusing power."*
> Jorge Ramos, Journalist and Author

Two close friends, Gary Schouborg and L. Pat Carroll approached us after reading Morgan's last book "Revelation and Healing: *A Father and Son Reunion"* and asked if we would consider writing more about Lionel Durand as a French Resistance fighter and as a combat reporter covering the

Algerian War of Independence. Our friends believed that there was a second book still waiting to be written about Lionel's life and times.

Lionel does deserve his own book. Unfortunately, he did not live to write it himself. So, we proudly present his story, highlighted by his own writing and recorded radio interviews and broadcasts, and in the memories of those who knew him best.

We recognized many corollaries between his times and our own. Several of the world's struggles that he reported on during WWII and the Cold War remain relevant to our society today. As such, we suspect that he would say to all journalists, especially to his fellow combat reporters: "Report the Truth, don't forget where you come from, and always get up when you are knocked down."

> *"To all the men and women of Newsweek and to the mountain climbers and statesmen, the actors, artists, writers, teachers, singers, diplomats and elevator operators who counted themselves his friends, Durand was more than a first-class reporter. He was kindness, resourcefulness, generosity, humor, and courage—and those are the qualities for which he will be missed."*
> The Editors of *Newsweek* January 23, 1961.

It is our hope that what we have written is a worthy tribute to a remarkable man.

1.Lionel Durand's Haiti: Then and Now

"Haiti is the eldest daughter of France and Africa. It is a place of beauty, romance, mystery, kindness, humor, selfishness, betrayal, cruelty, bloodshed, hunger, and poverty. Haiti is roosters crowing at dawn, drums in the night, coffee plucked wild from mountainsides, rum from ancient iron kettles, burning cane fields, dark sea, bright flowers, vast ruins and gingerbread houses. Yet romance and mystery, Haiti like any other, lie in the eye of the beholder. In that gaze

the real Haiti has for nearly two centuries been obscured by distance, prejudice, illusion, and misunderstanding."
Robert Debs Heinl and Nancy Gordon Heinl, "*Written in Blood, The Story of the Haitian People 1492-197*"

"*With no education, you have neocolonialism instead of colonialism, like you've got in (parts of) Africa now and like you've got in Haiti. So, what we're talking about is that there has to be an educational program. That's very important.*"
Fred Hampton, (1948-1969) Assassinated Chicago Black Panther Leader

"*I think Haiti is a place that suffers so much from neglect that people only want to hear about it when it's at its extreme. And that's what they end up knowing about it.*"
Edwidge Danticat (1969-) Haitian American novelist

The renowned American poet Hilda Doolittle (1884-1961) called Lionel Durand 'the Haitian' as did Lionel's friend, executive editor of *The Washington Post*, Ben Bradlee (1921-2014).

Lionel's story begins with his motherland: Haiti, *Ayiti*, 'the land of the mountains.'

"*They are affectionate people, free from avarice and agreeable to everything. I certify to your Highness that in all the world I do not believe there is a better people or a better country. They love their neighbors as themselves, and they have the softest and gentlest*

2

voices in the world and are always smiling. They may go naked, but your Highnesses may be assured that they have very good customs among themselves, and their cacique maintains a most marvelous state, where everything takes place in an appropriate and well-ordered manner.

No human eye has ever beheld a more beautiful land; nowhere is nature so immeasurably lush, so green, so untouched."
1492 Ship's Log (*The Log of Christopher Columbus*, translated by Robert Fuson)

Indigenous people, principally the Arawakan-speaking Taínos, were the Caribbean's inhabitants at the time of Columbus. Traveling by canoes from Central and South America, the Taínos arrived in Hispaniola (today's Haiti and the Dominican Republic) about 4,500 years ago. Fishermen enjoyed abundant fishing, and farmers cultivated vegetables such as yams, sweet potatoes, and cassavas. With complex hierarchical religious, political, and social systems which included forced labor and servitude of prisoners of war or captives of rival tribes, the Taínos had a thriving society and culture which would almost get erased by the Europeans.

In 1492 on the Bahamian island of Guanahani (San Salvador, present day Watling Island), newly arrived Columbus marveled at the Taínos, *naked as the day they were born,* living peacefully in Nature - so *untouched-lush-green.*

Kneeling on a beach on the north coast of Haiti, Christopher Columbus claimed Ayiti, renaming it Hispaniola for Spain and for Christendom. He wrote that he had never seen, in his twenty-three years at sea, such a large, protected harbor that could "hold all the ships of Christendom." (Cf. "The Taínos: *Rise and Decline of the People Who Greeted Columbus*" by Irving Rouse)

"   According to Columbus' records, over the next several days more than a thousand Taínos arrived to pay their respects to the visiting Spaniards, holding gifts above their heads: cotton cloth, parrots, cassava bread and fish, earthenware jars of water infused with aromatic seeds, and gold. For two days and one night, perhaps longer, the dates in the ship's log grow confused. The Spaniards did not sleep. In the log, Columbus made particular note of the Taínos women, who, he explained, were quite beautiful."
"The Gospel of Trees" Apricot Irving, pg. 67

Where did the Indigenous come from? What were their roots? There is strong evidence that the Indigenous peoples of the Americas, including those in Canada, USA, the Caribbean, Mexico, and Central and South America, came from Asia, crossing between 7,000 and 11,000 years ago, made possible with lower sea levels due to the accumulation of glacial ice. Beringia, a land bridge connecting northeastern Asia (Siberia) with northwestern North America (Alaska), made way for a monumental migration, spreading gradually for thousands of years over the continents.

Columbus wrote that the Taínos were "very well built, with handsome bodies and very good faces. They did not carry arms or know of them." Defenseless, the Indigenous were forced into slavery and made to mine for gold.

"Within twenty-five years of Columbus' arrival in Haiti, most of the Taínos had died from enslavement, massacre or disease. By 1514, only 32,000 Taínos survived in Hispaniola."

Sixty years after Columbus' arrival, it is estimated that most of the Taínos had died from slavery, violent treatment, and European diseases such as measles. The tragic 1518 smallpox epidemic killed 90% of the highly vulnerable natives.
(https://www.blackhistorymonth.org.uk "Taínos: Indigenous Caribbeans")

Over time, the Taínos intermarried with Africans brought to Haiti as slaves or on a much smaller scale with Europeans. The Taínos venerated their ancestors, whose spirits were a protecting bright presence in nature, including trees, water, and mountains.

Genetic studies have shown that there is Taíno ancestry in the modern populations of the Caribbean. Some Haitians, Puerto Ricans, Cubans, and Dominicans have Taínos mitochondrial DNA showing that they are Taíno descendants through the direct female line.

There are no pure Taínos, yet there are mixed ethnic heritage persons who proudly call themselves Taínos and who stay connected through the Taíno cultural traditions and arts. The history of the Taínos is being taught in Puerto Rican schools where children celebrate its culture through crafts, costumes, and dance. (Cf. "What Became of the Taínos?" *Smithsonian*, October 2011, Robert M. Poole)

.

The Taínos today are reviving and preserving Taíno language studies, beliefs, rites, myths, customs, arts, music, crafts, costumes, dance in appreciation for the harvest, esteem for the laborers, farmers, and fishermen and venerable ancestors as well as for contemporary inspiration to address wisely our contemporary problems. In Haiti and other Caribbean countries, there is growing interest in Indigenous ideas about sustainable living in a healthy environment and cooperative community. (Cf. *"Indigenous Resurgence in the Contemporary Caribbean: Amerindian Survival and Revival,"* Peter Lang)

About 95% of Haiti's population are of Black African origin, a minority are people of mixed European and African descent, a small number of European descent and an even smaller number of Syrian and Lebanese origin.

.

****

Lionel's African ancestors were brought in shackles to Haiti, slaves from the west coast of Africa. The French used slaves to work their cash crops of sugar, coffee, rum, indigo, and cotton. In the 1700s, built on the bent backs of enslaved Africans, Saint Domingue was the richest colony in the world. It was a desperately hard life, with the enslaved people working by hand and with machetes, shirtless in the unbearable heat on a sugarcane plantation, countless cuts by the sharp leaves, with perspiration burning their constant nasty flesh wounds, and ants biting them. The enslaved people suffered whips and dismemberment, hot pepper being rubbed in wounds, being hung and left to die. The enslaved lasted an average of three years before dying. The slave market boomed. From 1697 to 1804, eight hundred thousand slaves from Africa were brought to Saint-Domingue.

"By 1789, enslaved people outnumbered free people by almost ten to one in the colony. Out of a population of 556,000, there were about 32,000 White Europeans and 28,000 free people of mixed ancestry. The other five hundred thousand on Saint-Domingue were enslaved people of African descent." *"Haiti, Enchantment of the World,"* Liz Sonneborn, 2019

After the National Assembly of France approved the Declaration of the Rights of Man in 1789, a petition was sent to France calling for the granting of full citizenship to the mixed-race population of Haiti. In reaction to the call for equality of rights, the Whites in Saint-Domingue angrily beat and killed mixed-race people. Nevertheless, France, to the dismay of the local Whites, granted the mixed-race people equality if they were born of two free parents.

********.

"The most popular Haitian word in the world is zombie. And that's a reflection of the world more than it is of Haiti. I only came to Haiti in 1985 for musical inspiration. I only came for the rhythms initially. Then I found out that the rhythms don't walk alone. The rhythms walk with dance steps, with colors, with spirits, with prayer. The rhythms walk with God. With food-centered rituals to please spirits, Vodou is sort of like Thanksgiving, just several times a year. And it is feminist too, advocating equal status for male and female priests."

Musician Richard Morse (born 1957), owner of Port-au-Prince's Hotel Oloffson, raised in Connecticut by a Haitian mother and American father.

"Vodou is elusive and endangered but remains the soul of the Haitian people. Far from B-movie cliches, Vodou is a spiritual system and a way of life, but even in Haiti, where it became an official religion in 2003, it faces prejudice and hostility. Haiti, the saying goes, is 70% Catholic, 30% Protestant, and 100% Vodou, a spiritual system infusing everything from medicine and agriculture to cosmology and arts. Yet it is almost nowhere to be seen; ceremonies are not just expensive, but targets of hate crime. Jeom Frichenel Sisius, Haiti's principal Vodou priest, is a spiritual leader, doctor and midwife all at once. There are none of the corn flour drawings, animal sacrifices or rattles that characterize orthodox Haitian Vodou ceremonies, just a lot of dancing and ecstasy fueled by rum, drums and divine presence. It's almost full moon and is lured by the music and beauty of it all, the spirits. The 1920's and 1930's cinema, the heyday of B-films like White Zombie and pulp fiction, helped reinforce caricatures of Africans as hypersexualized, superstitious and demonic."
The Guardian, Kim Wall and Caterina Clerici, November 7, 2015.

Richard Morse's mother, Emerante de Pradines (1918-2018) was a 2nd cousin to Lionel. Richard was officially initiated into Vodou in 2001. For some 30 years, Morse's 13-member band has played soulful interpretations of Vodou prayers. On YouTube you can see Morse make music and reflect, openly critical of political corruption and violence in Haiti.

> *"Once in Haiti, Morse didn't know where to start. Soon after arriving (in 1985), the country went into political upheaval, and ruthless dictator Baby Doc Duvalier fled (in 1986). The military took over, and there were a lot of shootings.*
> *While immersing himself in Haitian culture and rhythms, an ongoing process that continues to this day, he had a dream: 'Someone came up to me and gave me a crazy message. I tried to investigate the dream once I woke up and went to Jacmel (an old port town), where I met Madame Nerva, a renowned Vodou priestess, who insisted I spend time with her.' The process of his initiation into Vodou began, culminating in his ordination as a priest circa 2001."*
> "How RAM's Combination of Vodou Culture and Politics Became the Soundtrack to Haiti's Modern History - A Stay in Haiti with Richard Morse" by Sharonne Cohen, May 25, 2016, www.vice.com)

The Vodou religion is not widely practiced in Haiti today, but in some small, inclusive, and welcoming communities, it still endures.

As with all religions, Vodou can be practiced in less benign and even destructive ways. President 'Papa Doc' Duvalier (from 1957-1971) famously fostered a personality cult that incorporated Vodou rituals to promote himself as a 'Vodou God' with absolute power over the people of Haiti.

****

In resolute rebellion, the enslaved took up arms ignited by the words of Vodou priest and rebel leader, Dutty Boukman, and priestess, Cécile Fatiman.

> *"The God who made the sun, who stirs up the sea and makes the thunder roar, is ordering us to vengeance. He will help us throw down the image of the colonist's God, for the Whites thirst for our tears. Listen to the freedom that is speaking to our hearts. I swear I will never let the blacks live in slavery."*

Vodou gave the spiritual voice to justify a rebellious response to slavery in Haiti and the throwing off slavery's iron chains.

On May 22, 1791, one thousand Blacks attacked 184 sugarcane plantations and coffee farms. There was burning, raping, killing, plundering, the beginning of a violent spasm of murderous rage in payback for the insufferable systematic violence meted out for over two centuries against the Blacks. Soon the one thousand grew to 20,000.

Black revolt terrified France, England, and Spain. In the United States, Thomas Jefferson "recognized that the revolution had the potential to cause an upheaval against slavery in the US not only by slaves, but by the White abolitionists as well." *US Department of State,* "The United States and the Haitian Revolution, 1791-1804"

Former slave Toussaint Louverture emerged as the leader of the fight for freedom from the French. In 1794, after France ended slavery in its colonies, Louverture switched his allegiance back to France. Next, he occupied the Spanish section of Hispaniola (now the Dominican Republic), declaring himself governor-general for life (an unfortunate precedent for coming military dictatorships in Haiti).

On November 9/10, 1799, Napoleon assumed complete power in France. He was determined to restore slavery to the empire. *The revolution is over. I am the revolution.* Napoleon sent 10,000 troops to Saint-Domingue in 1802; the French tricked Louverture into thinking they would negotiate peace, but instead they arrested Louverture, who died April 7, 1803, at age 59, in a freezing cell in Fort de Joux in the mountains of France.

The rebels "continued to fight without Louverture, under the leadership of Jean-Jacques Dessalines and Henri Christophe, and the rebel army finally defeated the French. On January 1, 1804, Dessalines officially announced that the French colony of Saint-Domingue was no more. It was now the independent nation of Haiti, the first modern-day state founded by formerly enslaved Blacks. Jean-Jacques Dessalines became Haiti's ruler. He ordered his army to kill all the French people still on the island, declaring himself Jacques I, the emperor of Haiti. In 1806, they assassinated the emperor." "Haiti, *Enchantment of the World*," p. 46

The country, though now free, was politically divided and in economic distress. Regrettably, in 1825 President Jean-Pierre Boyer was pressured to pay France a ransom of 150,000,000 francs for their lost properties (land and enslaved people) in exchange for France's recognition of the new and free country of Haiti. French ships patrolled off the coast of Haiti with orders to blockade Haiti if the payment was not agreed upon.

The human cost of Haiti's independence was staggering. Over 150,000 had died or 40% of the population, only 170,000 of the original 425,000 enslaved Blacks remained healthy enough to work and contribute to the rebuilding of the economy of the new state. With interests steadily compounding, it would ultimately take Haiti fully 122 years to repay France the ransom.

Although Haiti continues to face overwhelming economic and political struggles, it is, nevertheless, essential, vital even, to remember and acknowledge its remarkable historic past. For in the early 19th century, Haiti became the first independent Black republic in the history of the world after successfully overthrowing slavery and French colonial rule. Never, throughout the known history of humankind, has a nation of enslaved people ever successfully risen up, fought, and won their liberation entirely on their own.

****

1915-1934 US Occupation of Haiti

The USA occupation of Haiti began in 1915 when Haitian president Jean Vilbrun Guillaume Sam was assassinated, throwing the country into chaos. Woodrow Wilson sent 330 Marines to Port-au-Prince to occupy the country under the pretense of establishing political and economic order. The National City Bank of New York (now Citibank) had convinced President Wilson to take control of Haiti's financial and political policies, and $500,000 was transferred from Haiti's national bank to New York, and pro-American Philippe Sudré Dartiguenave was made President. A new constitution was written in 1917 allowing foreign land ownership; it was a time of forced labor, censoring of the press, and racial segregation. The US occupation lasted until 1934.

> *Over the course of the (Haitian) occupation, the attitude of the Americans was a constant source of bitterness that profoundly shaped the Haitian social experience. While there was some congenial contact between US troops and Haitians, there were also perpetual tensions, even at the highest level. In their daily lives meanwhile, Haitians often found the behavior of US troops racist, rude, and uncouth. One evening, a drunk marine threw rocks down on guests listening to a garden piano recital being given by a Haitian who had recently returned from studying at the Paris Music Conservatory. Haitians answered with violence, ending up in street fights with the occupying forces. Much of the tension involved what Haitians saw as a patent hypocrisy on the part of the occupiers regarding race and sex. At a reception for Franklin Roosevelt in 1917, for instance, US officers had danced with Haitian women but commanded their wives to remain in another room to avoid having to dance with Haitian men.*
> Laurent Dubois, "Haiti - *The Aftershocks of History"*

During the US occupation of Haiti, several American businesses were dominant in Haiti. The National City Bank of New York handled Haiti's finances and greatly shaped Haiti's economic policies. The United Fruit Company (now Chiquita) exported mainly bananas. Mining interest companies extracted mineral resources, such as bauxite, which was used in manufacturing aluminum. There were American owned sugar and coffee plantations, infrastructure development companies, and export-import companies.

In the *New Yorker* magazine article of July 28, 2015 "The Long Legacy of Occupation in Haiti," Edwidge Danticat writes:

> *I am writing this in Les Cayes, Haiti, where one of the worst massacres of civilians took place on December 6, 1929, during the nineteen-year American occupation of Haiti, an occupation that began a hundred years ago today. In my own family, there were many stories. My grandfather was one of the Cacos, or so-called bandits, who retired American Marines have always written about in their memoirs. They would be called insurgents now, the thousands who fought against the occupation. One of the stories my uncle Joseph used to tell me was of watching young Marines kicking around a man's decapitated head in an effort to frighten the rebels in the area. The notion that there were indispensable nation-building benefits to this occupation falls short, especially because the roads, schools, and hospitals that were built during this period relied upon a tyrannical forced-labor system. This occupation was never meant, as the Americans professed, to spread democracy, especially given that certain democratic freedoms were not even available to the United States' own black citizens at the time. During the nineteen years of the US occupation, fifteen thousand Haitians were killed. Any resistance to the centralized, US-installed puppet government was crushed.*

In 1922, Luis Borno took the presidency of Haiti. He increased forced labor and jailed critics. There was escalating resentment among the Haitians. The Les Cayes Massacre, in which between 12 and 24 Haitians were killed and 23 wounded by Marines while peacefully protesting the occupation, brought international attention. The Forbes Commission sent by President Hoover recommended local elections. A nationalist government was elected in 1930. They worked out an agreement for US withdrawal which was signed on August 7, 1933. The newly elected National Assembly then chose Stenio Vincent as President on November 18, 1930. In 1934, the last Marines left Haiti.

****

Louis Durand, Lionel's father, lived in New York City from 1911 - 1917. We know that he arrived from France in December of 1910 based on a December 4, 1910, New York City news clipping which noted that Haitian Consul General Louis Durand had negotiated a loan from France to Haiti.

Haitian Consul General Returns.

Among those who arrived yesterday on the French liner Savoie was Louis Durand, Haitian Consul General in this city. Durand is returning from Paris where he went in connection with the 25,000,000 francs loan to Hayti by the French government. Durand refused to discuss the matter.

What is so fascinating from this brief news 1910 clip is that it reveals that Louis Durand played an important role in attempting to manage the 85-year-old long fiscal distress and ever-growing national indebtedness inflicted upon Haiti by the original 1825 reparations ransom to France of 150,000,000 francs.

From 1910 to 1911, Haiti was in a state of political upheaval. President Simon, who took the oath of President on December 21, 1908, faced dire financial and political circumstances. This led to instability and a power vacuum with insurgent groups attempting to and ultimately overthrowing the government. Louis Durand, as the Haitian General Consul in New York City, played a pivotal role in the National Defense of Haiti when, in 1910, he brokered the purchase of and outfitted a large, state of the art yacht named *American* into a warship and ordered it to Cap-Haïtien to support the government of President Simon who was on the brink of being overthrown.

> *From New York, a July 20,1911 special in* The Washington Post*:*
> **Haiti Claims Armed Yacht - Said by Consul General to belong to the Government***.*
> *The arrival of the American big steam yacht at Cape Haïtien recalls the mystery surrounding her reported sale here about two weeks ago. Louis Durand, the Haitian Consul General in New York stated that* American *had been purchased by Haiti and was on her way to Haiti, laden with ammunition. It was sold some time ago by Mrs. Grace Watt Thomas to Evans R. Dick for $58,000. Mr. Dick, it was said, sold her for $258,000.*

More from the *Washington Post* July 20, 1911:
The yacht *American* Protects Foreigners at Cap-Haïtien, Will Halt Bombardment, Women Taken

Abroad after Rebels Capture the City: *Permission to use boat's weapons denied by US authorities. Anarchy reigns in Cap-Haïtien.*

Cap-Haïtien is in the hands of the revolutionists, and the sole protection of Americans and other foreigners at this port is the yacht American *which arrived here yesterday morning. The United States gun boat Petrel sailed from here several hours previous to the arrival of the yacht, leaving American interests unprotected, and when* American *came into the harbor, her owner, Evans R. Dick of New York found the town in a state of semi-anarchy. The insurgents were rapidly approaching.*

President Simon and his troops had left Fort Liberte for Port-au-Prince. Most of the residents took sides with the revolutionists, and soon the authorities were unable to check the disorders. Mr. Dick notified the officials that he would not permit any bombardments by Haitian warships and would protect the foreigners. Early last night, fighting broke out in the streets. The searchlight of the yacht was kept on the house in which the Americans, who were brought in from working on the railroad, had gathered with their wives. At daybreak, however, the government was overthrown: the revolutionists had occupied the town and streets filled with excited men and women shooting at random. All the American women were taken aboard the yacht, while the foreign consulates were filled with refugees. These included generals who had opposed the revolution. The French consul was slightly wounded.

Immediate Protection Claimed.

The whole American colony claimed immediate protection, and it is pointed out that serious results may follow if permission is denied the yacht owner to use rapid fire guns with which the vessel is supplied. Following the policy of the American government in preventing the bombardment of unfortified towns in Nicaragua and Honduras, particularly where heavy foreign interests may be endangered, the State Department has issued to the government of Haiti a mandate that the port shall not be fired upon.

During the July/August 1911 upheaval, President Simon ultimately fled the capital with his wife, children, and some followers; he took refuge on board the newly named Haitian cruiser *17 Decembre*, which formerly was the yacht *American*. Simon was waiting for a merchant vessel to take them to safety in St. Thomas, Dutch West Indies as his government fell to the rebels. (Cf. *New York Times* "Haitian Rebels Win: Simon now an Exile," August 3, 1911)

****

Overview of Haiti, 1920s to Present

Within Haiti itself, the thinker who truly defined the cultural awakening of the 1920s was the teacher and scholar Jean Price-Mars (1876-1969), whose writings became a touchstone for generations of Haitians. Haitians, he argued, suffered from internalizing the racist ideas directed at them by outsiders. In order to productively confront their social and political problems, they first needed to understand and accept that they were the equals of any other people. "Let us persuade ourselves that we are men like other men." Price-Mars urged Haitians to completely rethink the way they related to their culture. Haitians had a past, 'if not the most beautiful, then certainly the most engaging and moving in the history of the world, the transplantation of a human race to a foreign land.' And yet Haitians reacted with 'an embarrassment barely concealed, indeed shame,' when confronted with the fact of their African roots. A different Haiti is always, and still, possible, too.

Laurent Dubois, "Haiti - *The Aftershocks of History"*

In 1937, thousands of Haitians living in the Dominican Republic were massacred by Dominican troops. This severely strained relations between the two countries. As of 2024, the Dominican Republic is eight times as rich as Haiti, whose standard of living hasn't advanced since 1950. Facing economic challenges in 1941, Elie Lescot became the President of Haiti. Lescot's regime became dependent on foreign investments, especially from the United States. In 1946, a military coup overthrew Lescot, and Dumarsais Estimé assumed the presidency only to be ousted by another military coup in 1949. A year later after yet another coup, Paul Magloire (Kanson Fe), a lawyer supported by the Haitian military, the US, and the Catholic Church, was elected President of Haiti.

"The election of Magloire was the first in the nation's history where all adult males had the right to vote. During Magloire's rule, Haiti became a tourist spot for American and European tourists. His anti-communist position also gained favorable reception from the US government. In addition, he emphasized public works. Revenues from the sale of coffee were used to repair towns, construct roads, public buildings and a dam. He also oversaw the institution of women's suffrage. Magloire was very fond of a vivid social life, staging numerous parties, social events, and ceremonies. He amended the constitution to set, by referendum, a republican presidential regime and broke with parliamentarism. From 1954, Magloire's popularity fell. On December 12, 1956, Magloire's reign came to an end." (Wikipedia)

Hurricane Hazel ravaged southwestern Haiti on Columbus Day, October 12, 1954, leaving 100 dead and 100,000 people homeless. Funds intended to provide relief for the populace were often stolen before they could reach those in need...

****

"I was the first to have a pen in one hand and a gun in the other."
Jean-Claude Duvalier, Feb 2, 1971.

"A constitution is paper; a bayonet is steel."
Creole saying

The terrifying Duvalier Era began in 1957 with François 'Papa Doc' Duvalier. The only candidate, Duvalier was 're-elected' in 1961. In 1964, he declared himself President for Life. His term was characterized by violence, censorship, and human rights abuses. The Duvalier's censured or shut down media outlets to silence political opponents critical of their brutal regime. They embezzled state funds and foreign aid and forced Haitians to work on state-run projects without pay. In 1986, international pressure and demonstrations finally led to the departure from Haiti of Jean-Claude "Baby Doc" Duvalier.

****

In December 1990, a former Roman Catholic priest, Jean-Bertrand Aristide became the first democratically elected president in the history of Haiti. He was swept to power with the aid of a network of faith-based popular grassroots organizations. He earned two-thirds of the vote, defeating the internationally favored rival Marc Bazin, a former World Bank officer. Aristide attempted progressive reforms, reduced corruption, and trimmed state bureaucracy, and human rights violations were reduced to below previous levels. However, his action and populist stance seriously alarmed the elite and Aristide was soon deposed by a violent military coup just seven months after taking office. (refworld.org)

Three years of severe military rule followed Aristide, with reprisals against grassroots community activists, resulting in many fleeing the country, some crossing the border into the Dominican Republic, or heading directly or indirectly into other Caribbean territories, the US, and Canada, risking the dangers of rough seas. The US Coast Guard implemented a blockade against Haiti, intercepting refugee boats, sending those blocked back to Haiti.

Much of Haiti's infrastructure deteriorated during the three years of military control. An international embargo added to the full-blown crippling of the Haitian economy.

Aided by the US Marines, in 1994, Aristide again assumed power. However, many Haitians continued economic emigration to best provide for their families. So, wealth was mostly generated outside of Haiti, with too few internal economic opportunities and benefits for the people.

A year later, in 1995, René Préval was elected President of Haiti. The social, political, and economic dysfunction continued unabated. Then, once again, in 2001, Aristide was elected to lead Haiti. By 2003, in an attempt to further destabilize the Aristide administration, the US denied delivery, approved by the Inter-American Development Bank, to Haiti of US $500,000 social sector funds earmarked for health, education, and clean water for the poor marginalized majority of Haitians.

****

"The two main criminals are France and the United States. To become minimally civilized we should say we carried out and benefited from vicious crimes. A large part of the wealth of France comes from the crimes we committed against Haiti, and the United States gained as well. Therefore, we are going to pay reparations to the Haitian people. Then you will see the beginning of civilization." Noam Chomsky
"Even though the people there have so little, their attitudes resonate a crazy amount of love and joy. It is

truly inspiring to see that. My love for the country starts with them." Noah Munck

"Haiti, Haiti, the further I am from you, the less I breathe. Haiti, I love you, and I will love you always. Always." Jean-Bertrand Aristide

In 2002, President Aristide announced his intent "to pursue a claim against France to recover its Independence Debt." On behalf of Haiti, US attorney Ira Kurzban prepared legal actions against the French government to recover the estimated $21 billion (current money) extorted from Haiti during 1825 to 1944.

The legal process was cut short following the overthrow of the elected government of President Jean Bertrand Aristide on February 29, 2004. The subsequent coup government refused to pursue any claim against France.

It was Friday, February 27, 2004, the evening before the last day of Haitian democracy. The evening sun angled its refracting rays across the round room and altered the color and feel of the winding down. Jean-Betrand and Mildred Aristide sat hand in hand in the middle of the sofa in the middle of the room talking calmly and quietly to each other. They were not afraid and did not have a moment's misgiving over the course they had chosen. Profoundly spiritual people, they held in their souls a trust that they believed would survive the looming tumult. Though their people were materially poor, the Aristides recognized and prized in them the storied heroism of the Haitian nation and the measureless contributions its stoop-laboring people had made toward preserving the African self in the West. Haiti was home to the last heartbeat of the Middle Passage survivors' dimming memory of home. Ordinary Haitians believed this to be an ageless and immortal truth.

Randall Robinson, *"Haiti, from Revolution to the Kidnapping of a President, An Unbroken Agony"*

A catastrophic 7.0 earthquake on January 12, 2010, at 4:53 pm, 16 miles west of Port Au-Prince, tragically took the lives of 220,000 - 300,000 people. President Barack Obama responded: "We are just now beginning to learn the extent of the devastation, but the reports and images that we have seen of collapsed hospitals, crumbled homes, and men and women carrying their injured neighbors through the streets are truly heart wrenching. Indeed, for a country and a people who are no strangers to hardship and suffering, this tragedy seems especially cruel and incomprehensible. Our thoughts and prayers are also with the many Haitian Americans around our country who do not yet know the fate of their families and loved ones back home. You will not be forsaken. You will not be forgotten in this hour of greatest need. America stands with you. Help is arriving. Much, much more help is on the way. America's commitment to Haiti's recovery and reconstruction must endure and will endure. The losses that have been suffered in Haiti are nothing less than devastating and responding to a disaster of this magnitude requires every element of our national capacity."

The strongest storm, with winds up to 145 per hour, to hit Haiti in more than 50 years, Hurricane Matthew battered Haiti on October 4, 2016, taking an estimated 550 lives, leaving 1.6 million people in need of humanitarian assistance.

****

President Jovenel Moïse was assassinated by 28 foreign mercenaries, mostly Colombians, on July 7, 2021, at 1 am EDT. Ariel Henry, 71-year-old neurosurgeon, though never legitimately sworn in, assumed the role of acting President and acting Prime Minister on July 21, 2021. With the last election in 2017, the term of every elected official has expired so there is no legitimate leadership in Haiti today.

A 7.2 earthquake, 93 miles west of Port-au-Prince on August 14, 2021, took the lives of at least 2,250 with more than 12,200 injured. 650,000 people needed help. About 138,000 buildings were damaged or destroyed.

****

Spring 2024: Snapshot of the Obstacles on the Long Road to Haitian Self Determination.

> *The mental health crisis in Haiti is a silent epidemic, exacerbated by ongoing violence and a lack of adequate healthcare services. Without intervention, the psychological scars left by the current crisis will continue to affect generations to come.*
> Haitian Times, March 19, 2024

In response to the anarchy in Haiti, on March 4th and 5th, 2024 from 6 am to 5 am, Port-au-Prince was once again under curfew. The country continues to be plagued: 1.4 million Haitians on the verge of famine; 40% of the population without adequate food and water; around 155,500 Haitians displaced from their homes; armed gangs attacking the

National Palace and setting part of the Interior Ministry on fire; lethal violence, kidnappings, sexual assaults; attacks on the two largest prisons resulting in more than 4,000 inmates escaping into 80% gang-controlled Port-au-Prince.

Well-known Haitian activist, Monique Clesca, called it "days of terror, with armed gangs parading throughout Port-au-Prince and the police nowhere to be found." Clesca emphasized that Haitians want a Haitian-led solution to stopping gang-violence and quelling civil unrest.

On December 16, 2023, the Caribbean Community and Common Market (CARICOM), announced that for the sixth time, Prime Minister Ariel Henry and the opposition political parties could not settle the issue of whether Henry must first resign for Haiti to resolve its governance crisis. CARICOM group consists of 15 Caribbean countries coming together to form an economic and political community that works together to shape policies for the region and encourages economic growth and trade.

Finally, on March 12, 2024, CARICOM announced that Henry's resignation would go into effect after a transitional Presidential Council is in place. The transitional government in Haiti would select a prime minister and temporarily rule Haiti in order to abate the calamity.

The transitional council will include a representative from the following organizations: the Montana Group (civil society organization offering solutions to the crisis in Haiti); Haiti de France Collective (movement to promote democracy in Haiti and support Haitians in France who had to flee Haiti); Fanmi Lavalas (led by former Haitian President Jean-Bertrand

Aristide); Petit Dessalines (political party led by Jean-Charles Moïse); December 21 Group (coalition of business, civil, and political leaders); and EDE (political party of former Prime Minister Dr. Claude Joseph). Two non-voting observers will be chosen from the civil and the religious sectors. The council, still a shaky work in progress, pledges to re-establish public and democratic order in Haiti.

> *The Presidential Council has not been formed yet as the mediation and selection of representatives are still going on. Once the council is formed with a transferral of power, a roadmap can be decided upon. The gangs are terrorizing us. They went to the Chief of Police's house, and they looted it and set it on fire. This is what happened today. I don't know if someone is pushing the button for the gangs. These are questions all of us are asking. Poverty and inequality are endemic to Haiti. Perhaps endemic is not the right word but one should consider the root causes. So many Haitians are being displaced and facing hunger. We need to address the underlying structures, so this does not occur again. I am privileged. I have my garden of books. Imagine the ones who do not have food, do not have homes. It's a human catastrophe.*
> Monique Clesca (Montana Group), March 14, 2024, "Way Forward in Haiti"

On March 25, 2024, Dominique Dupuy, representing the EDE coalition stepped down from the Presidential Council due to safety concerns amid political attacks. A new representative will replace Dupuy. The council's official installation has been delayed despite two days of intensive discussions.

On April 1, 2024, CARICOM transmitted the definitive list of the members of the Presidential Council. After installing the Transitional Presidential Council, Ariel Henry's resignation will go into effect. The Council has the formidable task of first deploying a multinational mission to curb gang violence and then creating the peaceful conditions wherein fair elections can take place in 2025.

Newly elected US Ambassador to Haiti, Dennis Bruce Hawkins, is in Haiti to begin his diplomatic tenure and is supportive of the transitioning to a new government and installing the 9-member Presidential Council.

Although Ariel Henry and Kenyan President William Rutto recently authorized a bilateral agreement between Kenya and Haiti to deploy 1,000 Kenyan police officers to Haiti in order to halt the growing dominance of the gangs, the deployment of Kenyan police has subsequently been suspended. In response, Kenyan President, William Ruto, and Canadian Prime Minister, Justin Trudeau are now calling for international support of a multinational mission to end gang violence in Haiti.

On March 19, 2024, Jean Pillard, former Haitian ambassador in the UK, spoke to the Parliament urging immediate action, "to discuss the current plight of Haiti, a proud nation that stands as a testament to human resilience, its narrative complexly connected with trials since its bold proclamation of independence." Pillard stated that Haiti's political system has disintegrated. But a crisis can also be an opportunity for meaningful change. "The synergy between the global community and the unified spirit of Haitians, especially those in the diaspora, is paramount. Now is the moment to leave behind all that have underserved Haiti, in favor of innovative strategies, crafted by Haitians for Haitians, that truly align with its people's heart and spirit."

The Haitian Diaspora principally based in Miami, Boston, and New York City along with international faith-based organizations (FBO) and non-governmental organizations (NGO) continue to respond in order to help stabilize Haiti in the midst of its present social, political, and economic disaster.

As Lionel would no doubt remind each of us, we must continue to view Haiti from an all-encompassing perspective, careful to avoid limiting stereotypes and not giving into abject despair. Rather, we need to acknowledge the extreme complexities of the people's situation and, while continuing to respond to the immediate crisis, address the underlying causes of the severe trauma and distress in today's Haiti.

Haitians themselves are neither simple villains nor simple victims. More complex interpretations are few and far between. But the true causes of Haiti's poverty and instability are not mysterious, and they have nothing to do with any inherent shortcomings of the Haitians themselves. Rather, Haiti's present is the product of its history: of the nation's founding by enslaved people who overthrew their masters and freed themselves; of the hostility that this revolution generated among the colonial powers surrounding the country; and of the intense struggle within Haiti itself to define that freedom and realize its promise.
Laurent Dubois, *"Haiti - The Aftershocks of History"*

******

The Durand's Travel from Haiti to France

*I don't think that prejudice in France is based on color
or religion. It's based rather on the condition one is in
intellectually or socially. In other words, if a good man
happens to be a Negro in France, it does not make the
slightest bit of difference. There's been a long tradition
of liberalism, true liberalism in France for centuries.
France is one of the few countries where a man is free
first to find himself and then determine his own life and
destiny. He does not have to pretend to adhere to any
system or any manner of speech or religion or anything
like that in order to become a part of the 'free society.'
He can be a free man if he is free himself and has found
which way he wants to go.*
Lionel Durand, January 1, 1953 - Voices of Europe
Radio Interview
*There was never an American visitor who wanted a
glass of wine, or a wise briefing on French politics, or
a gay laugh in a bistro, who did not get it freely from
him. This was Lionel Durand.* Haiti Sun, January 29,
1961

Born in Port-au-Prince on December 22, 1920,
Lionel's Haiti was under the control of the USA. Lionel's
father, Louis Durand, was 57, and his mother, Madeleine de
Pradines, 28. At age 13, in 1933, Lionel and his family left
Haiti for a new home in France where his father served as the
last Haitian Consul to France before the war. Lionel spent the
rest of the 1930's as a diplomat's son in studies and ultimately
ended up at the Sorbonne when the war broke out.

30

Louis Durand "Papa Lou" Lionel Durand's Father

Madeleine de Pradines, Lionel Durand's Mother

2.Occupation and Resistance: Blacks Nobly Served

Lionel Durand, A Determined Man

"Nothing is lost for France. For France is not alone. She is not alone. The newly signed armistice (with Germany) will result not only in capitulation but also in slavery. Whatever happens, the flame of French resistance must not be extinguished and will not be extinguished. Long live a free and independent France." Charles de Gaulle, June 18, 1940, BBC radio

"France has lost the battle, but she has not lost the war." Charles de Gaulle

"The French Resistance cuts a wide swath in the public imagination, and not only in France. Books and films have planted indelible images of derailed trains and makeshift airstrips at midnight. These images reveal only a tiny part of the fluctuating, diverse, squabbling world of the French Resistance. Encompassing its whole range of activities is a challenge. In addition to sabotage, these activities included carrying two bamboo fishing poles (deux gaules —*a visual pun signifying support for Charles de Gaulle), scratching V for victory on walls, radioing intelligence to London, passing downed Allied airmen along a chain of safe houses to the Spanish frontier, printing and distributing clandestine news sheets."*
Robert Gildea

"In Paris, I found myself surrounded by Germans; they were all over the place. They played music, and people would go and listen to them! All along rue de Rivoli, as you could see from place de la Concorde there were enormous swastika banners five or six floors high. I just thought, "This is impossible. Imagine that someone comes into your home, someone you don't like, he settles down, gives orders. Here we are, we're at home now; you must obey." To me that was unbearable."
Pearl Witherington Cornioley, espionage-sabotage-reconnaissance agent for clandestine British SOE, Special Operations Executive, Second World War

"Humanity is one indivisible whole throughout space and time."
Paul Rivet, a leader of Groupe du Musée de l'Homme, a Resistance cell of intellectuals, scientists and lawyers.

The French army lost over 100,000 men before the Germans entered Paris on June 14, 1940. Millions of civilians fled to the south in the immediate chaos, but many soon returned. In July 1940, World War I hero Marshal Philippe Pétain was installed as Chief of State of the subservient Vichy government in the south and collaborated with the Germans. At the end of the war, Pétain was convicted of treason and sentenced to death, a sentence commuted by Charles de Gaulle to life imprisonment. Pétain died in prison on July 23, 1951. He was 96 years old.

On June 14, 1940, Hitler's army entered Paris with an overwhelming show of force. On June 23, Hitler, basking in the self-inflationary glory of the surrender of France, made his only visit to Paris.

Hitler made Napoleon's tomb among the sites to see. 'That was the greatest and finest moment of my life,' he said upon leaving. Comparisons between the Führer and Napoleon have been made many times. They were both foreigners to the countries they ruled (Napoleon was Italian, Hitler was Austrian); both planned invasions of Russia while preparing invasions of England; both captured the Russian city of Vilna on June 24; both had photographic memories; both were under 5 feet 9 inches tall, among other coincidences. But Hitler being Hitler, he came to do more than gawk

at the tourist attractions. He ordered the destruction of two World War I monuments: one to General Charles Mangin, a French war hero; and one to Edith Cavell, a British nurse who was executed by a German firing squad for helping Allied soldiers escape German-occupied Brussels. The last thing Hitler wanted were such visible reminders of past German defeat. Hitler would gush about Paris for months afterward. He was so impressed, he ordered architect and friend Albert Speer to revive plans for a massive construction program of new public buildings in Berlin, an attempt to destroy Paris, not with bombs, but with superior architecture. 'Wasn't Paris beautiful?' Hitler asked Speer. 'But Berlin must be far more beautiful. When we are finished in Berlin, Paris will only be a shadow.'
http://history.com, "Hitler takes a tour of Paris"; November 16, 2009

Initially, the French resistance to the Nazis was largely disjointed, localized, and primarily surfacing in the north and west of France. However, as the Vichy government expanded its cooperation with the Occupiers in the south through such acts as turning over foreign and French Jews to the Nazis and organizing recruitments of French laborers to work in Germany, the French Resistance began to take hold there too. While the French Army was defeated and about 1.8 million soldiers were taken as prisoners-of-war, General Charles de Gaulle began the arduous task of beginning the formal steps of establishing the Free French Forces in London to continue the fight to liberate France. In his historic and dramatic radio broadcast on June 18, 1940, he announced the presence of the

Free French Forces and the existence of the French Resistance within France to the world.

Nothing is lost for France. For France is not alone. She is not alone.

Lionel and others struggling against the enemy were inspired by the rallying words of de Gaulle to resist and fight. For November 11, 1940, World War I Armistice Day, commemorating France's World War I victory over Germany, university and high school students passed flyers calling for resistance: *November 11, 1918, was the day of a great victory - 11 November 1940 an even greater one!*

Here is an English translation of the handwritten French flier encouraging students to join the 11 November 1940 Arc de Triomphe demonstration:

French Students! *The 11th of November is the anniversary of the victory of right and liberty. The 11th of November is the symbol of eternal France. The 11th of November is the day of the dead, of our glorious dead. The 11th of November is the day of the living of our living hope. The 11th of November is the day of the nation, of the united nation. The 11th of November is the day of the youth, of the youth that does not accept the yoke of the invader and his accomplices. The 11th of November is the day of the revolt, of the revolt that will free us from the chains of slavery. 11th of November is the day of the fight, of the fight that will lead us to victory.*

French Students! *On the 11th of November, at 11 o'clock, in front of the Tomb of the Unknown Soldier,* *under the Arc de Triomphe, we will gather to honor the memory of our martyrs and to affirm our faith in the destiny of France. On the 11th of November at 11 o'clock, in all the towns and villages of France, we will demonstrate our solidarity with the prisoners, the hostages, the deportees, the patriots who suffer and die for the liberation of the fatherland. On the 11th of November at 11 o'clock, we will show the world that France is not dead, that France is alive, that France is fighting. On the 11th of November at 11 o'clock, we will say to the enemy: You will not pass! On the 11th of November at 11 o'clock, we will swear to be faithful to the spirit of the Resistance, to the ideals of the Republic, to the principles of the Revolution. On the 11th of November at 11 o'clock, we will say to the traitors: We will not forget! On the 11th of November at 11 o'clock, we will say to ourselves: We will win! Vive la France!*

signed by the National Union of Students of France (UNEF) and the General Federation of Students of Paris (FGEP)

Thousands of students pouring into the streets that day also threw stones as well as flowers. Jean Guéhenno: "Around 5:30 on Armistice Day, November 11, I saw German soldiers with bayonets charge at the students and throw them to the ground. Three times I heard machine guns firing." Around 150 students were arrested, beaten, and thrown in the Cherche-Midi Military Prison. Most were released in the weeks that followed.

There is a plaque in Paris at 156 Avenue des Champs-Elysées commemorating the start of the French Resistance:

"On 11 November 1940, the students of France protested en masse at the Tomb of the Unknown Soldier, the first act of resistance towards the occupiers."

Despite the risks involved, Lionel was probably involved and even arrested that day. We know that between 1940 and 1942 he was arrested twice by the Gestapo and escaped both times. We also know that he was a student at that time at the Sorbonne University and whose students played a large role in the November 11th demonstrations, occurring in broad daylight, this demonstration was the very first collective and public action of the Resistance. The Sorbonne would stay closed for one month.

Gathered at the Tomb of the Unknown Soldier at the Arc de Triomphe, the students and ordinary Parisians defied the Occupiers with a two-hour demonstration. Throughout the day, small groups laid bouquets of flowers, bound with French red-blue-white tricolor ribbons, at the foot of the Champs-Elysées statue of Georges Clemenceau who was the French prime minister in 1918 when Germany suffered its debilitating, bitter defeat. The French police confiscated the flowers, only to have more bouquets offered with a wish for freedom and for the defeat of Germany. 750 bouquets were counted that day.

The flame of French resistance must not be extinguished.

****

During the German Occupation of France, about 500,000 men and women participated in the Resistance. We proclaim as *presente* the Blacks, who did their part serving courageously in the Underground Resistance Movement in France. We honor in particular three Black men who were in the French Resistance - Addi Ba Mamadou, George Dukson, and Lionel Durand - and three distinguished and inspiring Black women - Jane Vialle, Eugénie Eboué, and the renowned Josephine Baker - each of whom contributed to the cause of French liberty.

The Durand's were living in the strategic port of Le Havre on the eastern side of the Seine Bay, which was captured by the Nazis in May 1940. The Le Havre Resistance was centered around branches of Le Havre High School and the Vagabond Bien-Aimé (Beloved Vagabond), both involved with British Intelligence and acts of sabotage up until the Normandy Invasion on June 6, 1944.

The besieged people of Le Havre had to suffer food and other shortages, bombings, censorship, arrests, and political anti-Semitism. Resistance fighters—small cells of women and men, some armed—fought against the Nazis and the collaborative Vichy Regime by broadcasting intelligence to London, writing underground newspapers, which Lionel most certainly must have helped with (the pen being mighty aside the sword), and indicating escape routes for Allied soldiers caught behind enemy lines. These fighters also sabotaged electrical power grids and telecommunication networks.

"Resistance workers carried out thousands of acts of sabotage against the German occupiers. The risks were great. More than 90,000 resistors were killed, tortured or deported by the Germans. They also gathered intelligence and helped Allied airmen and prisoners of war escape the country, risking their lives to save the young strangers." (https://nzhistory.govt.nz/war/d-day/the-resistance)

****

Like other students, Lionel knew the dangers of joining the resistance. A teacher of French literature described the fate of student-resistors during the Occupation: "Imprisoned, tortured, deported, executed,or killed in combat, my students bore witness, through their suffering or death, that we were not mistaken: that the vague thing we had talked about together, anxiously yet fervently – freedom exists; and

40

that humanity in the universe and in history is only after all, a sort of honorable plot to spread that freedom and preserve it. I will never believe that men are made for war. But I know they are not made for servitude, either." ("*Diary of the Dark Years, 1940-1944, Collaboration, Resistance, and Daily Life in Occupied Paris,*" Jean Guhénno, p xxxii)

We know from Lionel's 1953 radio interview on Voices of Europe (chapter 6) that Lionel was in the intelligence-gathering section of the Underground from 1940-1942, which broadcast intelligence to General de Gaulle in London. The Germans drove around in their cop-cars, searching to arrest the sources of radio waves broadcasting to London.

Lionel Durand most likely used a different name, careful to protect his family from his involvement in the Resistance. He knew that he and his family would be in great danger if he were captured.

****

It took a while for the Resistance to have some serious bite. The seeds were planted by the determined, defiant, clandestine, liberty-loving members of the Resistance. But the seeds took time to sprout vigorously.

Before 1943, military resistance in France was nearly nonexistent...The surprisingly good behavior of the German army in France also prevented the growth of an early resistance...German soldiers did sporadically loot abandoned estates and farms during the campaign of 1940, but in general, their behavior, as insisted upon by their superiors, was proper... The biggest problem for the early resistance within France however was that none of the great organizations chose to espouse it. The Church, the army, the political parties, and the unions all remained silent. The only group that might have been able to effectively coordinate resistance was the French Communist Party, or PCF."

Military Resistance in France 1940-1944," Matthew McDole, University of Virginia B.A. thesis April 2005.

****

From the beginning, there were some prominent thinkers who participated in the French Resistance. When in 1941 the Nazis publicly executed famous Communist anti-fascist journalist Gabriel Peri, renowned existentialist philosopher and pacifist Albert Camus joined the French Resistance, not as military personnel but as a writer-editor for *Combat* magazine. It was his way of *pushing back*, of finding strength within to overcome oppression, to write rebelliously in the midst of Nazi hateful aggression.

In the midst of hate, I found there was, within me, an invincible love. In the midst of tears, I found there was, within me, an invincible smile. In the midst of chaos, I found there was, within me, an invincible calm. I realized through it all, that in the midst of winter, I found there was, within me, an invincible summer. And that makes me happy. For it says that no matter how hard the world pushes against me, within me, there is something stronger—something better pushing right back.

Counterfeit identification papers for Jews were forged and printed by members of the Resistance. Under the Vichy government, French authorities and police identified and rounded up tens of thousands of Jews, arrested and packed them in trains headed for Auschwitz and other concentration camps. On an October 29, 2017, airing of the 60 Minutes TV interview, Adolfo Kaminsky, 92 years old, told his story of day and night printing of fake identification cards, passports, food ration cards, birth and marriage certificates for Jews, especially children, to be hidden in convents, schools, and farms or smuggled across the border. Learned while working at a dry cleaner, Adolfo became one of the most expert forgers in France during the war. He produced fake documents and, along with Resistance networks, helped save as many as 14,000 Jews. Adolfo was 18 years old when he joined the Resistance.

"Jewish sounding names had to be replaced with more French-sounding ones, and the word Jew had to be somehow erased. We had to move very quickly and help these people disappear before they were arrested. So, it was just racing against the clock and actually I called it racing against death."

****

One cannot yet speak of military effectiveness in the French Resistance at the close of 1942. Although some isolated sabotage operations were carried out by SOE (Special Operations Executive) the spectacular destruction of the electrical station at Pessac, for example - by and large the resistance was without arms or support from the general population. Paris

was not a dangerous place for a German soldier. 1941 remains the seed time of the resistance. While no militarily effective resistance yet existed, the nucleus of what could one day become true was present in the movements and SOE networks. The population, confronted with the reality of German reprisals, also found it more difficult to treat the war as a matter of no concern.
"Military Resistance in France 1940-1944," Matthew McDole

Groupe du Musée de l'Homme (Museum of Mankind), an organization of intellectuals, scientists and lawyers, led by Boris Vildé (1908-1942) and Paul Rivet (1876-1958), started to publish a clandestine bulletin, *Résistance,* urging the French people to fight against the German occupation. Director Rivet's Musée de l'Homme was the only museum which remained open after Nazi tanks invaded Paris early morning of June 14, 1940.

"The Musée de l'Homme tacked a freshly placed French translation of Rudyard Kipling's poem, *If,* to its doors: *"If you can keep your head when all about you are losing theirs...you'll be a Man my son!"* It was a defiant gesture, a dangerous message and even a sly call to arms. Unbeknownst to the invading army, the man behind the sign, the museum's director (Paul Rivet) became a moving force in the nation's secret counteroffensive network. He boldly criticized racist ideas promoted by many anthropologists (and adapted by the Nazis) and was an outspoken critic of anti-Semitism." *Smithsonian* magazine, "The Museum Director Who Defied the Nazis" by Laura Spinney, June 2020

The Gestapo began to hunt down those responsible for underground newspapers, mostly members of the Communist and Socialist parties. Many of them, along with escaped soldiers of the French army, fled to the forests of the unoccupied zones. They organized themselves according to political beliefs and geographical areas, eventually joining together to form the Maquis.

Boris Vildé was executed by the Germans in February 1942. But Boris, with his galvanizing underground publications had left a trail which, if followed, would lead to France's democracy.

****

But the Resistance movement sputtered at first:

Resistance had so little appeal in 1940 that even those most threatened by the occupation - France's 200,000 Jewish citizens - largely eschewed it. Parisian students who staged German protests by celebrating the armistice of 1918 were gunned down in the street. A nineteen-year-old boy who cut German telephone lines was apprehended and summarily executed. Even a young French sailor found tearing up German posters was sentenced to three months in jail. To the satisfaction of the German authorities, France would remain largely quiet until the summer of 1941. With attacks on the rise, reprisals became the order of the day in France, and many innocent Frenchmen were killed. The most flagrant incident occurred on October 21, 1941 when communists assassinated a German

colonel. Hitler was incensed and ordered the shooting
of 100 to 150 hostages. Forty-eight were executed.
"Military Resistance in France 1940-1944," Matthew
McDole

At the beginning of German occupation, French Jews,
with some notable and inspirational exceptions, considered
themselves as citizens of the French Nation first and Jews
second. They did not for the most part associate with the over
100,000 Eastern European Jews who streamed into France in
the 1930's to escape the deadly Nazis.

When the Third Republic was shattered by the German
blitzkrieg attack in the early summer of 1940, there were
approximately 350,000 Jews in France. Less than half of them
were French citizens. Many of them were endangered refugees
who had fled the murderous Nazi persecution in Germany.
(US Holocaust Memorial Museum)

At least 75,670 Jews were deported from France to
concentration and extermination camps; of the 69,000
sent to Auschwitz, 2,570 survived. Some of those
deported passed through multiple camps. Another
3,000 Jews died in French internment camps. US
Department of State, The JUST Act Report: France

Even when the Vichy started to persecute foreign Jews,
many French Jews thinking they were safe, looked the other
way, as did the majority of their countrymen. Yet some Jews
did take part in the Resistance from the very beginning.

Jews were among the founders of the Musée de l'Homme network in 1940 which published underground news...Moreover, Jews of long standing in France, while feeling themselves distinct from Jewish immigrants, were often tied to families beyond French borders. Contact, sometimes direct, with Jewish refugees from Germany no doubt rapidly sharpened the sense of politically astute French Jews as to the true nature of Nazism...The Jewish Communist press was already significant in the 1930s...It was necessary to wait for the 1970s and the ripening of French memories of WWII, the Vichy government (collaborative French State, July 10,1940-August 9, 1944), and the Shoah (Holocaust) before the Jewish contribution to the Resistance gained even minimal recognition in France.

Tablet, "Was the French Resistance Jewish?" Reneé Poznanski, May 2, 2016

By 1944. The OJC, Organisation Juive de Combat (Jewish Fighting Organization) took part in a military campaign against the retreating German army. They captured a German train full of soldiers, food, and weapons. Wearing Star of David armbands, they announced to the German prisoners: *Ich bin Jude* (I am a Jew).

Bernard Musmand (1930-2010), a Jewish partisan, posed as a Catholic at a boarding school and became a courier for the Sixieme, a resistance group in Rodez, France. He transported falsified papers for Jews fleeing Nazi persecution. At age 14, he became a member of the Maquis and participated in two major battles against the Germans. He was made a second lieutenant in the French army but given a desk job.

Bernard often came face to face with Germans or with French sympathizers but knew how to act confident and had a trick: to ask for the time or a match in perfect German. This eased any suspicions others might have of his true identity. His youth and his chutzpah saved him countless times. "It was an exciting time, in certain ways, " Bernard remembered. "I wish and hope it will never come back, but everything counted, and you felt life was precious."
jewishpartisans.org, "Partisans & Countries"

After the war, Bernard refused, to ever after, utter any words in the German language.

****

The Durand's in New York City, 1942: Lionel Lands Job at Voice of America

Lionel and his parents and sister had to flee France for their lives in the summer of 1942. In the US National Archives, we discovered as part of a wartime special investigation by the FBI, a report which states, filed under the signature of J. Edgar Hoover, the first Director of the Federal Bureau of Investigation (FBI, 1924-1972), that Lionel's father, Louis Durand, the Haitian Consul in Le Havre, France had returned to his home in Le Havre on July 16, 1941 and encountered four German soldiers who demanded his passports and those of his family. The soldiers refused to give him a receipt for the passports and confiscated the following: diplomatic passports and passports of Durand's family; exequatur and act of nomination by Haitian Government;

marriage certificate of Durand's son, Lionel and Yolande; official and private letters; all consular seals; blank passports; and notes belonging to Durand's son and a photograph." The Durand family were now without any diplomatic identification papers to protect them in occupied France. It was urgent that Lionel and his family leave Nazi-occupied France.

On June 22, 1942, Lionel Durand left France on the S.S. Drottningholm, Lisbon to New York City, with his father Louis Durand (born 1863), his mother Madeleine de Pradines (born 1892), sister Andrée, and Lionel's "wife" Yolande. Lionel is erroneously listed as single on the 1942 ship's manifest while Yolande is listed as being married. *(National Archives and Records Administration, List or Manifest of Alien Passengers for the United States)*

After arriving in New York City in late June 1942, Lionel was hired by Voice of America to broadcast ("I have experience.") *the truth* to France, using the opportunity to greet his family members still there.

'The Voice of America' was a vital project of the Office of War Information (OWI), which oversaw the US propaganda efforts during World War II. OWI would create many books, pamphlets, Hollywood films, other media and, of course, radio broadcasts, domestically and internationally. Voice of America began operation on February 1, 1942, with a broadcast from West 57th Street in New York City to Germany. Arriving in New York City five months later on June 30, 1942, Lionel, who had already been working in intelligence from France, was quickly appointed French section director of Voice of America.

****

"We look forward to a world founded upon four essential human freedoms: freedom of speech, freedom of religion, freedom from want, and freedom from fear."
Franklin D. Roosevelt, January 6, 1941, annual message to Congress

"Propaganda warfare is not merely a battle of words. It is a battle for people's minds and through their minds their physical actions."
John Houseman who established Voice of America in February 1942 as an aggressive tool of warfare.

Working the French Desk at Voice of America in New York City, Lionel continued to serve the Resistance in Occupied France. The Voice of America's contribution to the Resistance is made clear in "The Voice of America: Propaganda and Democracy, 1941-1945" by Holly Cowan Shulman.

In February 1942, when the Voice of America first went on the air, the Allies were losing the war. The summer of 1942 witnessed a crucial turning point for wartime France as Germany began subjecting the French to the increasing rigors of the wartime economy, rationing food, deporting massive numbers of Jews, and, finally, in September, instituting the hated *releve*, or relief system. The Nazi government, short of manpower, began staffing factories with foreign workers.

During the winter of 1941-42, the French voluntarily contributed nearly 150,000 such workers, who at the time were seeking better wages and working conditions than they could find at home. But French enthusiasm did not last, and by the spring of 1942 there were very few French workers willing to go to Germany.

The existence of the Resistance, the Voice now implied, demonstrated that France was at war on the side of the Allies. No longer was France neutral. France was resuming its natural position, as the spearhead of European resistance to the domination of the Germans. By the summer of 1943, the Voice was reporting acts of sabotage within France which, by their very size and success, constituted propaganda for resistance. Accordingly, they began distinguishing between covert acts of sabotage whose authorship the Germans would not be able to uncover and overt activities that could bring swift vengeance. The Voice declared: *"In every country oppressed by Germany, resistance is growing. The German recruiting agents double their efforts to hire workers from the occupied countries. But the workers know that when they go to work in Germany, they are neither more nor less than civilian prisoners. The workers of Lyon have addressed a new appeal to the French people, to exhort them to resist the Nazis and to sabotage the German war machine by every means at their disposal."*

The Voice began to define the Resistance as French preparation for the coming Allied invasion. In June 1943, the propagandists dropped the term *resistance* and substituted in its place *the movement of liberation. France can be liberated only by the total military defeat of the Axis power and the driving of the Axis invaders out of French territory.*

Lionel Durand and shipmates arrived in New York City, late June 1942

When Lionel, his wife Yolande, and his sister Andrée arrived in New York City with their father and mother, Louis Durand and Madeleine de Pradines, the ship's manifest reported that their closest relative was Lionel and Andrée's older brother René, who was still living in France. Two of René's children, Michel and Micheline, tell stories in Chapter 8 about Lionel and the Durand family in New York City, Haiti, and Paris. Andrée made her way back to Haiti where she lived most of her life.

René Clarence DURAND

A young René, Lionel's brother, Morgan's uncle

Andrée Maillard, wife of René Durand

René stayed in Paris during the war to work with his father-in-law in the field of selling precious woods and to take care of his young family. René and Andrée Maillard would ultimately become the parents of six children: Michel, Micheline, Jacques, Claude, René, and Camille.

****

Lionel's Marriage Annulled

Lionel's first marriage on June 15, 1941, to Yolande Françoise Bemova (1920–2005), was arranged, *a marriage blanc*, to enable his bride to escape, for unknown reasons, from Vichy France and get to the US; records show they did not live together after they arrived in New York City. In fact, Yolande was living on Park Avenue. The marriage was annulled on August 17, 1945, by the Supreme Court of New York. Yolande needed the State Department to confirm the annulment so that she could access her father's estate in France. She had renounced her French citizenship for Haitian citizenship as a requirement of her marriage to Lionel.

On July 17, 1947, a lawyer for Yolande Françoise Bemova, Lionel's first "wife, "detailed her difficulty in obtaining her family inheritance in France:

> *Honorable Sirs:*
> Yolande Françoise Bemova, *my client, has consulted me concerning her difficulties in connection with the matter of her rights in her father's estate. He,* François Bem, *was a French National, and died in France, leaving his estate to his widow Josephine Marie Bem*

and my above-named client. My client married Lionel Durand, a Haitian citizen at Paris, France, renouncing her French citizenship, and entered the United States as a Haitian national under diplomatic status, as Lionel Durand was then connected with the Haitian Consul at Le Havre, France and later connected with the Haitian Consul in New York, N.Y.

On May 14, 1945, she obtained a decree of annulment of her marriage to Lionel Durand, and last month she married an American citizen.

In order that she may receive her father's estate without the intervention of her first husband, it is necessary for her to have to have the said decree of annulment recorded by the French Office of Civil Status. I am advised by French counsel that she must obtain the transcription of the annulment of the marriage.

****

Blacks Nobly Served in the French Resistance

Given France's increasing demographic weakness in comparison to Germany, the thought of raising a large army of black Africans in the defense of the French mainland became more attractive in the first years of the twentieth century.

Raffael Scheck, "They Are Just Savages: German Massacres of Black Soldiers from the French Army in 1940"

Little has been said about non-white resisters who were among the 200,000 men and women from the colonies...The question of racial identity was clearly a factor for the French Resistance...The French colonies across Africa, Asia, and the Caribbean were central to the Allies and the Free French...People of color were at the very heart of numerous resistance activities in the metropole from the very onset of the Occupation in the summer of 1940.

Ludivine Broch, "Colonial Subjects and Citizens in the French Internal Resistance, 1940-1944"

In May and June of 1940 when the German army was fighting in France, they encountered Black African soldiers who had been recruited by the French army. For the most part, German troops treated White POWs according to the mandates of the Geneva Convention (1929). Being Black however, "they are just savages" was dangerous, as Blacks were considered subhuman. "Germans dealt with the Black Africans in a way that anticipated the horrors of the racialized warfare associated with the later German campaigns in the Balkans and the Soviet Union. In close combat, German units fought against Black soldiers of the French army with a ruthlessness that suggested that no prisoners would be taken. On many occasions, Black prisoners of war were shot, sometimes up to several hundred at a time. When Germans did not kill Black prisoners outright, they often separated them from the White French captives and subjected them to harsh treatment. The Journal of Modern History, "German Massacre of Black Soldiers from the French Army," R. Scheck, 2005

"There were about 2,000 Black fighters, individuals of African descent who participated in the French Resistance. (See the GR16P Resistance Fighter database of the *Service Historique de la Defense in Vincennes*). By 1937, there were about 82,000 North Africans, mostly Algerians, in France. "Resistance network files in the National Archives in Paris do contain lists of members and general testimonies that can provide clues as to the names of colonial participants in the French internal Resistance." (Ludivine Broch, "Colonial Subjects and Citizens in the French Internal Resistance, 1940-1944)

****

Guinean Addi Ba Mamadou (1916-1943), known to the Germans as "the Black Terrorist," was a member of one of the first Resistance cells, the Maquis des Vosges (a range of low mountains in Eastern France). Sharp-shooting rifleman, Addi Ba had worked as a cook in France since 1933. Addi Ba soon became a most wanted menace for fighting the Germans in Eastern France. Imprisoned on June 14, 1940, he later escaped from a POW camp in the Vosges.

Protected in the small village of Tollaincourt by villagers and using counterfeit identification, Addi Ba lived openly as a hired farm worker. "The fact that local villagers later testified that Ba's presence in rural Vosges, along with that of other demobilized soldiers did not raise much suspicion amongst either the French or the German authorities, indicates that the French population was more racially diverse during that period than might be depicted or even imagined in the post-war period. It is essential that the image of who was a Resistor be diversified to better reflect the reality of this period and to speak to France's contemporary multicultural reality."

(https://frenchempireww2.wordpress.com, "Black Terrorist-18 December 1943," Nina Wardleworth (Dr.), December 18, 2017)

Addi Ba helped smuggle Jews and people of color into Switzerland. The safeguarding and transporting of Jews and people of color was a necessary contribution by citizens, from the beginning of the French Resistance. Addi Ba is the subject of a 2017 film, *Nos Patriotes*, Our Patriots, directed by Gabriel Le Bomin. It is an historical drama based on Addi Ba's life with its challenges, contributions, sacrifice, and bravery. Addi Ba fights for the French Resistance despite initially experiencing prejudice; soon he is embraced wholeheartedly as a hero by the villagers.

In Addi Ba's time, a degree of racial discrimination existed in France. The attitude toward, and treatment of, Blacks varied depending on the context, location, and the individuals involved. France, however, was further ahead on this issue than the US which had a deeply entrenched political and social system of racial segregation and discrimination. Many African American soldiers who served in Europe found the French society and people more welcoming.

In Britain and the US, Black American soldiers faced severe prejudice. Lucy Bland's 2019 book, *Britain's 'Brown Babies,'* documents the impact and long-term social challenges that resulted when "approximately 240,000 Black American service members were stationed in Britain between 1942 and 1945. An estimated two thousand children were born as a result of relationships that were formed with British women. These mixed-race children were routinely stigmatized and called 'half-castes' by the British, and 'Brown Babies' by the American Black press."

Bland's research shows that in race and class-conscious Britain, the children who were raised by their birth mothers and/or their grandparents fared the best outcomes overall, but nevertheless they also experienced the same social stigma and discrimination as those children who were not raised by their birth mothers or their grandparents. The ongoing social stigma and discrimination which these children faced made it almost impossible for them to be adopted. The majority of them, sadly, were left to be brought up in institutional settings. The racial discrimination against these children was first established by the US military's policy of refusing to allow Black service members permission to marry the White mothers of their babies. This was in stark contrast to the estimated one hundred thousand WWII 'GI War Brides' of White service members who were allowed not only to marry, but also to emigrate to the United States with their children.

****

"A trawl through the GR16P Resistance fighter database of the *Service Historique de la Defense in Vincennes*, has revealed that there are at least 2,000 colonial Resistance fighters who received formal Force Français de l'Intérieur accreditation. Another 200–300 colonial Resistance fighters have been identified through the *Mémoires des Hommes* database and the database of the *Maitron des fusillés et executes*.

These Colonial Resistance fighters come from every French territory." (https://frenchempireww2.wordpress.com, "Black Terrorist-18 December 1943" Dr. Nina Wardleworth, December 18, 2017)

Addi Ba was romanticized in the 2012 novel, *le Terroriste noir* (The Black Terrorist). His courageous short life left plenty for the author's adventurous imagination. Though exaggerated in the movies and the novels, the French cultural norm is still one of honoring and respecting the memory of the Resisters.

Addi Ba was arrested on November 18, 1943, tortured, and killed at Epinal along with the Maquis leader, Marcel Arburger. Thanks to the efforts of local inhabitants of Tollaincourt, on July 13, 2003, Addi Ba was remembered and eulogized with honor and affection, and was posthumously awarded the Resistance Medal.

****

On August 26, 1944, George Dukson was one of the few Blacks at the parade to celebrate the August 25, 1944, end of Nazi rule in France. "It is 3 pm on Saturday, 26 August 1944. Paris is liberated. Under a blazing sun, General Charles de Gaulle, in full dress uniform, is standing at the Arc de Triomphe. He is at the head of a massive parade...Caught up in the enthusiasm of the moment, George Dukson, convinced that he had as much right to be there as anyone else, Dukson had simply invited himself on to the head of the parade. His presence was completely unscripted, a piece of spontaneous bravura, and it was soon snuffed out by protocol. Newsreel rushes show Dukson being unceremoniously kicked off the march, at gunpoint... Despite being a true representative of the Resistance rank and file, he had no place in de Gaulle's demonstration...Dukson was not the only African in the Resistance. Of the 1,030 members of the Order of the Liberation created by Charles de Gaulle, 14 were African. Hundreds of other black people played vital roles in the struggle. Most are long forgotten."

"The Lost Lion of Paris: The Extraordinary Story of George Dukson," independent.co.uk, August 12, 2009

"Black Lion of the 17th Arrondissement," Georges Dukson (1922-1944), was a charismatic fighter for the French Resistance. René Dunan told Dukson's "magnificent and sad" story of this native of Gabon, a French colony. Dukson joined the French Army (just as his father had done in 1914) to be a soldier in Europe where he was captured just before the Occupation in 1940. By October 1942, about 20,000 French West African soldiers were fighting for de Gaulle's Free French Army. After two years, Dukson escaped from Nazi imprisonment and "found his way to Paris, a wanted fugitive."

On June 6, 1944, the Allies' storming of Normandy ignited an uprising in which Dukson participated as leader in a Resistance cell. Fighting valiantly, he disabled German trucks and killed an enemy tank driver, "gleefully posing on that captured tank and a photo of him latched onto a surrendered German soldier."

Dukson became somewhat of a Paris celebrity, written and talked about, caricatured and toasted in bars, cheered in public and hailed in restaurants. Signed photos of Dukson sold for 100 francs; photos of de Gaulle were 15 francs.

Allied High Command were wrong to assume that Parisians would be hostile to Black fighters. It was the Allied High Command of the United States, England, and France that showed their prejudices and who wanted only White faces to soak up the glory and public adulation of defeating Germany.

On August 26, 1944, Dukson had been one of the few Blacks at the parade to celebrate the August 25, 1944, end of Nazi rule. He had his brief moment in the Paris sun that day, even if de Gaulle, himself, wouldn't allow him to bask in it for long.

At the end of the war, driven by financial difficulties, Dukson resorted to running a black-market operation in Paris where he was arrested. He tried to escape, was shot and died at the tender age of 22.

****

Black women, such as Jane Vialle (1906-1953) and Eugénie Eboué (1891-1972) made praiseworthy contributions to the conquering of the Nazis.

Jane Vialle, daughter of a French father and African mother, was born in the Republic of the Congo. Her father returned to France when Jane was seven years old. She became a journalist.

At the start of the war, she moved from Paris to Marseille and became an intelligence agent in information services, just like Lionel Durand, with one of the three principal Resistance movements in the South of France. With Resistance fighters' help, she was sprung from a Nazi prison. "In January 1943 she was charged with treason, tried, and convicted. She was incarcerated for four months in the Brens women's concentration camp and then transferred to the Beaumettes women's prison in Marseille until December 1943. Some sources, including the French government itself, indicate that Vialle escaped from prison." (*Black Perspectives*, "From Concentration Camps to the Senate: Black Women in the French Resistance," Annette Joseph-Gabriel, March 13, 2017)

****

Eugénie Eboué was born in French Guyana and married Félix Eboué in 1922, a "power" couple of substance. Félix Eboué (1884-1944) was a French Guianese politician who served as a colonial administrator. In 1940, he rallied and coordinated support for Charles de Gaulle's Free French Forces. He published *The New Indigenous Policy for French Equatorial Africa* which championed respect and appreciation for African traditions, development of existing social structures, and the betterment of working conditions. He was the first French Black man to be assigned to such a high post in the French colonies.

Eugénie received the prestigious Medal of Resistance. "At the start of World War II, she joined the Women's Army Auxiliary Corps and was stationed as a nurse at the Brazzaville military hospital until 1944. Her contributions to the war effort and subsequent political activism earned her at least twenty-six medals of recognition." ("From Concentration Camps to the Senate: Black Women in the French Resistance")

Both Eugénie and Jane were voted to serve in the French Senate where they addressed the problems of colonialism and advocated for legislation that would protect the rights of women in France's colonies.

Vialle "pursued legislation that would change France's paternity laws in order to increase state protections for otherwise unrecognized mixed-race children and by extension their African mothers. Both were active in a Black internationalist project and made connections between liberation struggles in Africa, the Antilles, and the United States. During her time in the United States, Vialle was the NAACP's guest of honor and was also featured in what was known then as a Negro History Week kit. She was the only woman in a lineup of Black internationalist figures, including Carter G. Woodson, W. E. B. DuBois, emperor Haile Selassie, and Felix Eboué." ("From Concentration Camps to the Senate: Black Women in the French Resistance")

****

Josephine Baker (1906-1975) was a shining Black star of the French Resistance and the Human Rights Movement.

"Americans, the eyes of the world are upon you. How can you expect the world to believe in you and respect your preaching of democracy when you yourself treat your colored brothers as you do? The things we truly love will stay with us always, locked in our hearts as long as life remains...You must get an education... You

must go to school, and you must learn to protect yourself with the pen, and not the sword."
Josephine Baker

"Surely the day will come when color means nothing more than the skin tone, when religion is seen uniquely as a way to speak one's soul, when birth places have the weight of a throw of the dice and all men are born free, when understanding breeds love and brotherhood... More is achieved by love than hate. Hate is the downfall of any race or nation."
Josephine Baker

I imagine Lionel Durand met and enjoyed performances by the celebrated Jazz Age dancer, singer, actress and undercover spy for the Resistance, Josephine Baker. At Paris cafes, Ernest Hemingway (1899–1961) enjoyed libations and conversations with the vivacious Josephine, calling her "the most sensational woman anybody ever saw. Or ever will."

"I wasn't really naked. I simply did not have any clothes on."
Josephine Baker

Eavesdrop for yourself as you read this passage from the book, *Hemingway in Love: His Own Story* by A. E. Hotchner, who recorded Hemingway's stories about his shaky love life. It should be noted that when Hemingway gave this interview, he was staying in the New York City psychiatric ward at St. Mary's Hospital in Rochester, Minnesota. Just a few weeks after this interview, he died from a self-inflicted Scott double-barreled 12-gauge gunshot wound to the head.

"I couldn't take my eyes off a beautiful woman on the dance floor—tall, coffee skin, ebony eyes, long seductive legs: Very hot night, but she was wearing a black fur coat. The woman and I introduced ourselves. Her name was Josephine Baker, an American. Said she was about to open at the Folies Bergère, that she had just come from rehearsal. I asked why the fur on a warm night in June. She slid open her coat for a moment to show she was naked. 'I just threw something on,' she said, 'we don't wear much at the Folies. Why don't you come? I'm headlining as the ebony goddess.' I spent that night with Josephine, sitting at her kitchen table, drinking champagne sent by an admirer. I carried on nonstop about my trouble. . . Josephine listened, intense, sympathetic. She was a hell of a listener. She said she too had suffered from double love. The rest of that night, into dawn, we talked about our souls."

No wonder Lionel's friend, Picasso, was so attracted to draw paintings of the alluring Josephine. Jean Cocteau, who later also would become friends with Lionel Durand, was instrumental in making Josephine a star.

But her life as a child was difficult and filled with neglect and abuse. Josephine grew up in St. Louis, Missouri never knowing the identity of her biological father. She later reflected, "St. Louis represented a city of fear, humiliation, misery and terror...A city where in the eyes of the white man a Negro should know his place and had better stay in it." At age 13, Josephine was living on the street in a cardboard shell, dancing on street corners for meager coins. Yet by 1925, at the age of 19, she was sailing to Paris, fleeing poverty and "the terror of discrimination." Josephine was on her way to conquering Paris and audiences throughout Europe, embarking on a 50-year career.

Josephine's close friend and famous writer of her day, Colette (1873-1954), described one of Josephine's early performances: "We love her assured, penetrating, emotional voice...and we do not tire of the gentleness, that affecting desire to please...African Josephine covered by a white woolen oriental cape, and swathed in veils...her eyes huge, outlined in black and blue, gaze forth, her cheeks are flushed, the moist and dazzling sweetness of her teeth shows beneath dark and violet lips..."

"Agent Josephine American Beauty, French Hero, British Spy," Damien Lewis, pg. 18

Josephine was the first Black to have the leading role in a major motion picture, *Zou Zou,* in 1934. She became a star of the Folies Bergère and La Revue Nègre. She would later face some prejudice when on tour in Europe where Hitler's racist ideologies were growing; she once rode in a carriage to her hotel as protestors against her performance lined the streets. The scene reminded Josephine of the race riots that had "shaken her community when she was a child."

There was no stopping Josephine Baker; in 1930, in Paris, she recorded her emotional signature song *J'ai Deux Amours* (I have two loves). In 1937 she became a French National Citizen.

****

On September 1, 1939, Hitler invaded Poland. The Soviet Union invaded Poland on September 17th. They divided between them a broken and devastated Poland . . . The garrison of 182 Polish soldiers returned fire on the 3,000 Germans. . . What lay in store for the teenage Bik at the end

of the 27-day war in Poland was an experience in a wartime slave operation. "The sound of bombs and explosions broke into my town and destroyed it. The horrors of war followed; people were beaten, tortured, executed by firing squads, or hung in the streets. For a teenage boy, these things were unthinkable." Shortly after the United States entered the war, Bik was conscripted by the Nazi SS and taken to work in forced labor. Bik escaped from forced-labor camps twice and in 1944 was arrested as a political prisoner for doing so. "With wire around my wrists, I was thrown into a boxcar and transported to Gross-Rosen concentration camp." Liberated from Bergen-Belsen concentration camp, Bik says he tells his story with the hope that people will listen and do everything in their power to prevent such things from happening again."
The Herald-Tribune, "70 Years after Invasion, a Polish Survivor Remembers," Catherine A. Hamilton, September 1, 2009

As a response to Hitler's Invasion of Poland, in 1939 Josephine Baker was recruited by French military intelligence. In 1937, Josephine had married Jean Lion who was Jewish. "It gave her double the reason to abhor and to fear the ascendency of Hitler and his ilk."
"*Agent Josephine - American Beauty, French Hero, British Spy*," Damien Lewis, pg. 20

Josephine was to get vital information, such as the location of German troops, from the loosened lips of partying Japanese and Italian military leaders, enchanted by Josephine at their embassies. In 1940, Germany entered Paris and Josephine, at the insistence of Jacques Abbey, head of the counter military intelligence, fled to southern France, where she opened her house to members of the Free Forces, providing them visas.

French Jesuit priest, anti-Nazi war hero, Father Victor Dillard would "endeavor to get the first wartime intelligence dossier into Josephine's hands. For his efforts to combat the rise of the Third Reich, Father Dillard would be murdered at Dachau concentration camp."
"Agent Josephine American Beauty, French Hero, British Spy" Damien Lewis

Father Dillard rallied and organized French workers to oppose the Compulsory Work Service, *Service du Travail Obligatoire* (STO), the forced deportation of hundreds of thousands of French for Hitler's war effort. Both men and women were required to enlist under the laws of Vichy France rather than from German mandates.

"A total of 600,000 to 650,000 French workers were sent to Germany between June 1942 and July 1944. France was the third largest forced labor provider, after the USSR and Poland, and was the country that provided the largest number of skilled workers."
"When Paris Went Dark: The City of Light Under German Occupation, 1940-1944" Ronald C. Rosbottom

In January 1943, Father Dillard joined young French workers who were forced to go to Germany as slave laborers. He pretended to be a married electrician and worked in a ball bearings factory in Wuppertal. He was arrested by the Gestapo for his defense of fellow workers and sent to Dachau where he was killed after six weeks on January 12, 1945.

"Victor Dillard, SJ: Spiritual Resistor and Apostle to the STO Slave Laborers in Germany: Martyred at Dachau," Monsignor Philippe Verrier

As an entertainer, Josephine Baker could travel to neutral countries such as those in South America or Portugal. She carried documents to be sent to de Gaulle in England. Notes were written in invisible ink on her sheet music.
"Jazz Cleopatra: Josephine Baker in Her Time" Phyllis Rose, 1989

On August 19, 1961, Josephine received the Croix de Légion d'honneur, highest order of merit for military and civilian action. Josephine accompanied Dr. Martin Luther King Jr. on his 1963 March on Washington, the only official woman speaker. In her speech, she acknowledged Rosa Parks and thundered to the captivated audience, "I have walked into the palaces of kings and queens and into the houses of presidents. But I could not walk into a hotel in America and get a cup of coffee, and that made me mad, and when I get mad, you know that I open my big mouth. And then look out, 'cause when Josephine opens her mouth, they hear it all over the world."

3. *Newsweek* Collaboration: Lionel and Ben Bradlee

Lionel and Toto (Irène)

Lionel returned to Paris in 1956 for Newsweek. *It was during the four years that followed that he established his reputation as a correspondent who understood*

*both the people he was reporting on and the people -
the American people - he was reporting to. As a former
member of the Resistance, he knew most of the major
figures of that heroic era up to and including President
de Gaulle. As he was also the intimate of art figures,
including Pablo Picasso, and of the directors of the
Paris Opera, M. Durand wrote magazine articles for
many American publications on the Paris art, music
and cultural scenes.*
New York Times, January 15, 1961

*"Lionel and Toto (Irène) Durand were at my wedding
party. . . Lionel Durand was one of the most
remarkable men I ever met. He was my* Newsweek
*'assistant,' which does him no justice at all, since he
was twice as smart as I was about most things,
certainly about all things French."*
Ben Bradlee

Ben Bradlee (1921–2014), close friend with John F.
Kennedy, played an important part in Lionel's professional
and social life. In 1956, Ben Bradlee, *Newsweek's* post-war
Paris bureau chief, hired him.

In "*Conversations with Kennedy and A Good Life:
Newspapering and other Adventures,*" Bradlee expressed his
appreciation for Lionel. "To be blunt about it, I didn't know
anything about blacks or the black experience, and I was about
to become involved in the leadership of the number one
newspaper in a city (Washington, D.C.) that was 70 percent
black and a readership that was 25 percent black. I had only
one black friend as a grown up, my *Newsweek* colleague,
Lionel Durand, in Paris."

Bradlee continued: "Lionel used the French familiar to Picasso. He knew the leaders of the burgeoning French film industry, the literary shots big and small... incredibly well connected, especially to the cultural scene, where I struggled. He was a fabulous asset to me and to *Newsweek*. We traveled to the Place des Vosges, trailing tin cans from our car, courtesy of Durand who knew full well that the French had no such custom. And we drank bottle after bottle of champagne, toasting the miracle we had pulled off and the start of our great adventure."

In 1951, Ben Bradlee was the assistant press attaché in the American embassy in Paris. He covered the French protests after the conviction of Ethel Rosenberg and Julius Rosenberg. "They were convicted of giving the Russians information vital to the manufacture of atomic weapons. The trial, the verdict, and especially the death sentence had been absorbed then inflamed France...The American presence was overwhelming; American cash was everywhere and the Rosenberg's being the symbolic rallying point for everyone who had a bone to pick with our government. Not just the Communists, who lived on anti-Americanism, but the intellectuals, the Socialists, and everyone who worried about McCarthyism and the death penalty."

Bradlee remembered his first meeting with JFK at a Georgetown dinner party: "I sat next to Jackie...We came home together, and by the time we said good night, we were friends, comfortable together and looking forward to the next time...When I got to know Kennedy, I kind of staked him out as part of my own territorial imperative, and as he prospered, so did I...little by little it was accepted by the rest of the

Newsweek Bureau and by New York that Kennedy was mine. If a quote was needed, I was asked to get it, and without really understanding what running for president entailed, or where it would all end, I embarked on a brand-new journey. Nothing in my education or experience had led me to conceive of the possibility that someone I really knew would hold that exalted job. The field in front of him was filled with mines. His age - at forty-three, he would be the youngest man ever elected president, the first one born in the twentieth century. His religion - too much of America believed that a Catholic president would have to take orders from the Pope in Rome. His health - he had been referred to by India Edwards, chairman of the Citizens for Lyndon B. Johnson National Committee, as a 'spavined little hunchback.' His father Joseph P Kennedy's reputation was secure as a womanizing robber baron, who had been anti-war and seen as pro-German while he was Ambassador to Britain during World War II, and pro-McCarthy during the fifties." (*The Good Life*, 1995, pg. 205)

Newsweek's Ben Bradlee received the plum assignment of covering Kennedy as he traveled throughout the USA during his candidacy for President. And when Kennedy won, "There was an invitation for supper that night with Jack and Jackie at the Kennedy's house in the Kennedy compound...We arrived early, Tony eight months pregnant, and were greeted by Jackie in the same condition. Kennedy came downstairs a few minutes later, and before anyone could say anything, he smiled and said 'Okay, girls. We won. You can take the pillows out now.' Over drinks we talked nervously about what we should call him, 'Mr. President sounded awesome, and he was not yet President.'" *The Good Life*, 1995, pg. 212

Bradlee was devastated when his friend JFK was killed and rushed to be with Jaqueline Kennedy at Bethesda Naval Hospital where the President's body had been taken. "There is no more haunting sight in all the history I've observed than Jackie Kennedy, walking slowly, unsteadily into those hospital rooms, her pink suit stained with her husband's blood. Her eyes still stared wide open in horror. She fell into our arms, in silence..." *The Good Life*, 1995 pg. 259

Bradlee went on to become the managing editor, then executive editor of *The Washington Post* from 1965 to 1991. Considering that Lionel had extensively covered the French war and occupation of Vietnam in the 1950s, we are confident that Bradlee would have enlisted Lionel, if he had lived, to continue to write about Vietnam in the 1960s as America escalated the war.

In the 1970s, Bradlee, as the executive editor, oversaw the work of two *Washington Post* young reporters, Carl Bernstein and Bob Woodward, as they investigated the 1972 Watergate scandal, the burglary at Democratic Party headquarters. The *Washington Post* would win a Pulitzer Prize for its 400 articles about Watergate over 28 months. President Nixon resigned under the threat of impeachment in August 1974.

Bradlee received the French Legion of Honor, the highest award given by the French government, at a ceremony in Paris in 2007. On August 8, 2013, President Obama named

Ben Bradlee the recipient of the Presidential Medal of Freedom.

****

Working at *Newsweek* with Ben Bradlee and his co-workers was the apex of Lionel's robust career. *Newsweek* was a popular magazine covering politics, news, and culture among a wide variety of topics. In a smooth transition for Ben Bradlee, *The Washington Post Company* acquired *Newsweek* in 1961 and remained in its ownership until 2010.

Newsweek's **1956-1961 Correspondent and Paris Bureau Chief, Lionel Durand**

Newsweek

Spotlight on Business } **OUR COMPACT CARS**
The Score Now

FEBRUARY 8, 1960 25¢
[INDEX—PAGE 13]

France's de Gaulle: The Final Crisis?
(Special Six-Page Section)

Lionel's fingerprints are all over the February 8, 1960, *Newsweek* special six-page section about Algeria, "France's de Gaulle: The Final Crisis?" Lionel not only took the magazine's cover photo of de Gaulle, but he collaborated with Ben Bradlee and fellow writers to produce the momentous story.

At what would become the last year of his short life, Lionel was continually reporting on the Algerian War of Independence (1954-1962), starting with this *Newsweek* coverage on February 8, 1960, and his last cables being published on January 26, 1961.

The war precipitated intense violence and human rights abuses. The French army was viciously oppressive, yet the Algerians fought back. Lionel bravely entered the fray and conducted the following interviews.

We read the entire piece, the original *Newsweek* issue in hand, and found it fascinating and electric. In it, we learned more about de Gaulle and the ongoing Algerian War for Independence. The special six-page section carries Lionel's byline in interviews that he conducted from the personal perspective of a French Army Colonel, a Settler and a Moslem Worker.

Newsweek had planned to devote the magazine cover to the boom in compact cars, but, because of the decisive time in Algeria, the editors rushed out a revised cover 'of the man whose prestige now rests on saving the Fifth Republic - Gen. Charles de Gaulle.'

****

On January 8, 1959, Charles de Gaulle was inaugurated as the first president of the Fifth Republic in which executive power was increased while the National Assembly's power decreased. De Gaulle was firm in his resolve that Algerians would have the free choice of their future. "That is the only policy that is worthy of France."

In February 1960, Algeria was embroiled in the bitter war. The key players in Lionel's story are de Gaulle, the French settlers (colons), Muslim Algerians, and the French Army.

De Gaulle promised to end the crisis in Algeria. Four generations of French settlers had lived in Algeria. Fearing the loss of their economic and political power, the settlers staunchly opposed Algerian independence. The Muslim Algerians, the majority of the population, faced discrimination and human rights violations and were determined to win the war. The French Army attempted to suppress the uprising through military force.

De Gaulle shifted France's policy toward Algeria with a September 16, 1959, speech outlining a proposed referendum in which Algerians would determine their own future.

But it wouldn't be easy for de Gaulle, Lionel reported, as the stakes were high. "Four generations of Frenchmen (the settlers) have sweated and toiled to make Algeria French." France was investing $600,000,000 a year in Algeria, Africa's largest country by area, which was rich in oil and minerals and guaranteed shipping lanes through the Mediterranean Sea. There were almost a million French settlers in Algeria which had a total population of 11,277,757.

"Frenchmen threatened to destroy the Republic, and plunge Algeria into civil war. The French Army had wavered in its loyalty and the settlers of Algeria had talked of secession from France. Yet one great towering figure had imposed his will on the crisis. This man could now be called the greatest Frenchman of the twentieth century: his name was Charles de Gaulle."

The interviews conducted by Lionel were titled "Algerian Grass Roots—Confused Loyalties, Doubts, and

Hopes." How did individuals with varied interests living in Algeria react to de Gaulle's crisis? To find out, *Newsweek's* Lionel Durand interviewed an army colonel stationed in a garrison in eastern Algeria, a 45-year-old settler who was a mechanic in Algiers, and a Moslem construction worker from Oran.

Lionel conducted face to face interviews in the midst of the turmoil. He offered a balanced and nuanced view from starkly different perspectives.

****

Army Colonel

Lionel Durand: Where do you stand in this crisis?

Army Colonel: I feel torn because my comrades and I have a job to do— fighting the National Liberation Front (FLN)— and instead we are being drawn into a political conflict.

LD: What do you think of the political conflict?

AC: I see it as a fight between Frenchmen of Algeria who want to remain French and Paris politicians who don't know what they want but are prepared to give up Algeria.

LD: Has the sense of discipline diminished in the army?

AC: In the field, not at all. But the army has been made an important factor in the political life of the nation, not always with its consent. Some feel we must take sides.

LD: Is the French Army obeying orders?

AC: On the whole yes, but only up to a point. There are orders which the army would not obey. For example, we would refuse to fire on the French population - the so-called insurgents. We don't feel it is wrong for Frenchmen to demonstrate in favor of France.

LD: If you had to choose between loyalty to General de Gaulle and keeping Algeria French, what would you do?

AC: I frankly don't know. We have all been thinking about this. Our mission here is to keep Algeria French by fighting the FLN. Now we are told we must let the Moslems decide about independence. I do not think de Gaulle will sell out Algeria—he is a patriot and a great Frenchman. But he must take a clear-cut position in favor of keeping Algeria French.

****

French Settler (colon)

LD: What do you think of the insurgent leaders?

French Settler: We don't care who the leaders are. We care about the idea: we want to keep Algeria French.

LD: Would you consider secession to keep Algeria French?

FS: It won't come to that point. France cannot live without Algeria. And maybe we couldn't live without France.

LD: Do you believe the settlers can impose their will on the French nation?

FS: We are not trying to force anybody to do anything. But if Algeria ceases to be French, I might as well become a Cuban.

****

Algerian Moslem (Muslim)

LD: What do you think of the insurrection?

Algerian Moslem: I understand little about French politics, but I think de Gaulle is trying to help us Moslems.

LD: Are you for the FLN?

AM: You don't know my name so I can tell you that I pay a monthly tax to the FLN collector. But I do it mostly to live in peace.

LD: How would you vote in a free Algerian election?

AM: Maybe for independence. But I think it's better to have good relations with France—as long as we have real equality. The settlers will never give us full equality. Maybe de Gaulle will

4.Lionel, Jean Cocteau, and Pablo Picasso

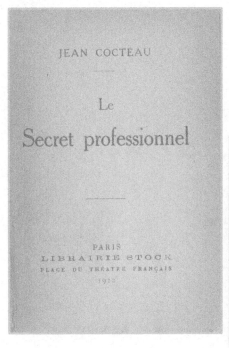

Jean Cocteau, A Natural Treasure of France

Cocteau's book: *"Le Secret professionnel,"*
Illustrated/inscribed for Lionel '*my friend'*...

Jean Cocteau's Letter to Lionel in French

"Life is a horizontal fall."
Jean Cocteau (1889-1963)

"How sinister when a man is saluted like a god."
Jean Cocteau reacting to Hitler in 1938

The social milieu in which Cocteau had been raised had no tradition of resistance...Come what may, a writer's vocation is to write, not get mixed up in politics...His distant utopia was a world without judges or police, without borders or nations, where painters, poets and musicians lived together in harmony with acrobats, muses, and boxers.
"Jean Cocteau, A Life," Claude Arnaud

"Lionel Durand knew the leaders of the burgeoning French film industry, the literary shots big and small."
Ben Bradlee

Jean Cocteau's and Picasso's response to the French Resistance was complex and sometimes quite different. Although Picasso didn't actively participate as a member of the French Resistance; he spoke out in strong opposition to the Nazi regime and supported his Jewish friends as well as members and activities of the French Resistance. Cocteau, though rarely and based principally on personal and artistic connections, did associate with Resistance members, even at times offering his home and using his connections to help individuals in need. He had been influential in helping bring Josephine Baker to prominence. However, Cocteau - famous for his poetry, visual arts, and cinema - remained associated with a "sophisticated collaborationist gang of chic socialites and celebrities," whereas Picasso primarily belonged to the "circle of surrealist writers, artists, and clandestine Resistance activists."

Jean Cocteau served as a member of the Comité de la Cinématographic which oversaw the film industry. Cocteau made a film, *La Belle et la Bête* (Beauty and the Beast), a traditional French fairytale that was commissioned by the Vichy Government. Visually interesting, whimsical, and poetic, the movie was widely acclaimed, but its production was also criticized as being supportive of the Vichy Government.

Back in the 1920s, Cocteau had actively participated in social anti-Semitic tropes fed by Christian prejudice. But by the 1930s, he reversed his course of thinking and actively disavowed his earlier anti-semitism: "Shake the hands of our Jewish comrades."

Courtesy of Lionel's grandson, Lionel Changeur, here is the English translation of Cocteau's letter to Lionel seen above in French:

23 February 1958

My Dear Lionel Durand,

I am very pleased with your letter. You know about the wall of rigidity and a particular inflexible morality that exists between us and a lot of people.

Since you've come through the door, we'll have a nice chat.

I'm leaving Paris on the 3rd or 4th. You'll have to pass by 36 rue de Montpensier (75001 Paris) before then. Between half past noon and 1:30 pm.

Either we'll have a quick meeting, or we'll make a firm appointment.

Your Jean Cocteau

****

On June 14, 1940, German soldiers occupied Paris, home of Lionel, Jean and Pablo. Jean Cocteau fled Paris to the south joining the exodus of two million refugees.

He returned in September, renting an apartment in the heart of the city in the Palais-Royal. "They (the Germans) didn't like the Jews, as everyone knew, or the Slavs, but the Parisians - the sons and daughters of Renoir and Toulouse-Lautrec - they loved…The cabarets and risqué bars, the Moulin Rouge and the Boeuf sur le Toit, the brothels and the gaming rooms - all reopened by the dozens…France may have lost half of its territory, but Paris was still the capital of the world." (*Jean Cocteau A Life*, Claude Arnaud, pg., 616)

German bands would regularly and triumphantly march through the principal streets of Paris. French dailies (all censored) continued to be published and placed on the newsstands alongside glossy German magazines.

By the fall of 1940, rations had begun. "Cigarettes, sugar, and chocolate were the first to become scarce, as well as coal for heat and cooking gas. Cocteau was warned that ties to far-off colonies (Indochina in particular) were weakening, and the opium supply would be tapering off…By early 1941, Cocteau had managed to completely kick the opium habit." (*Jean Cocteau A Life*, Claude Arnaud, pg. 627)

Pablo Picasso as a Political Artist

Lionel and Pablo Picasso deep in conversation in his Paris Studio. In background: Picasso's 1954 *Portrait of Jacqueline Roque with Her Hands Crossed*

Musée Picasso-Paris, Paris, France

> *'Picasso's first word was "piz" short for "lápiz," the Spanish word for "pencil"; it's like Picasso was born an artist'* https://www.pablopicasso.org

> *"I am determined to do it (paint* Guernica*). We have to arm ourselves for the war to come."* Picasso, 1937

"There was a large group of people. It was like seeing the room of a great matador with his court of admirers all around him as he shaves...Two frequent visitors to the rue des Grands-Augustins in these years were Picasso's poet friends, Jean Cocteau and Paul Éluard, who represented different sides of France's political and ideological spectrum. Cocteau had sided with the sophisticated collaborationist gang of chic socialites and celebrities. Éluard, on the other hand, belonged to the circle of surrealist writers and clandestine Resistance activists."
Michel Leiris, describing the ambience of Picasso's Paris studio in 1942

Immediately before the outbreak of the war in 1939, Pablo Picasso left Paris for southern France and returned to Paris in August of 1940.

Picasso (1881–1973) was an affectionate friend of Lionel and Lionel's wife, Irène, and their young daughter Barbara, who in 1959 wrote a letter to Picasso, which is archived at Picasso Museum and Foundation, *Musée Picasso-Paris*.

****

You can view a whimsical spirited gift, a Lion(el) sketch from Picasso to his friend appearing as the front cover of this book. With it, Picasso himself is inviting the reader to explore the life, work, and times of his Haitian friend, Lionel Durand.

Lionel did the French translation of a book, *The Private World of Pablo Picasso,* written by David Douglas Duncan. Duncan, a renowned photographer and author of *This Is War,* first met the 75-year-old Picasso while he was taking a bath. Invited into the home and private studio of Pablo, Duncan had three months' access and shot over 10,000 photos, selecting three hundred of them for the book that Lionel translated into French. Lionel's grandson, Lionel Changeur, has the books (French and English) in his treasured possession.

In the future, Lionel's 10 letters and his daughter Barbara's letter to Picasso will be available to the public. These letters certainly are going to be revealing. The documents - Lionel Durand (10 pieces) 1956-1960 and Barbara Durand (1 piece) 1959 - were in the possession of the French National Archives ("residing within their holdings"), but recently were sent to the Picasso Museum and Foundation, Musée Picasso-Paris. In 2022 the Musée Picasso-Paris launched an extensive programme to process the archives it now has in its custody, with a view to the forthcoming opening of the *Centre d'études Picasso.* This study center will offer the optimal conditions for accessing the Museum's resources and will provide a privileged setting for scholarly exchanges within the research community. The archives are not searchable at the moment. As work on the archives is ongoing and challenging, no specific date can currently be given when researchers will then be able, for example, to make available digital copies of Lionel's and Barbara's letters.

****

Lionel, Pablo, and Paris! Such a fascinating relationship must have served to have fortified Lionel's creative juices as a journalist, not to mention an exhilarating component of his own social, artistic, and intellectual life. *"As he was also the intimate of art figures, including Pablo Picasso, and of the directors of the Paris Opera, M. Durand wrote magazine articles for many American publications on the Paris art, music and cultural scenes." (New York Times,* January 15, 1961)

When *Newsweek* did a picture story on Picasso's London exhibition, Pablo supplied his own captions for Lionel's photographs. "I did this," explained Picasso, "out of friendship for Lionel."

The 1956 movie, *"Le mystère Picasso,"* ("The Mystery of Picasso,") directed by Henri-Georges Clouzot, takes us into Pablo's studio where we are invited to participate as Picasso creates paintings for the camera, fresh before our eyes, images pouring into our senses and expanding our consciousness. We see Picasso in one scene - smoking a cigarette, in shorts, sandals, no shirt - drawing one black curve after another: "For the first time, the daily and private drama of the blind genius will be experienced publicly. In the darkness of the canvas, the light slowly appears." Who can say what Muse was 'guiding the creator through his perilous adventures?' Picasso reflected the unconscious source of creativity in a close up shot of his entranced eyes: "One would die to know what was on Rimbaud's (master poet) mind when writing a poem." Wanting to keep the paintings limited only through viewing the film, most of the paintings were destroyed.

****

Pablo Picasso was at the cultural epicenter of Paris from 1900 (when 19) until he left for the Riviera in 1967. He and Lionel were happily Frenchmen by choice.

In the summer of 1987, Morgan visited Museo Reina Sofia in Madrid, Spain to see Picasso's 1937 heart wrenching, antiwar oil painting, 11- ft. tall and 25.6 ft. wide masterpiece, *Guernica*. Picasso presented in bleak gray-black-white colors the horror inflicted on the Basque city of Guernica, which was bombed and machine-gunned (from low-flying planes) by the Nazis in April 1937 during the Spanish Civil War. The Nazi airstrike destroyed three-quarters of the city, killing over fifteen hundred civilians and maiming hundreds more. Guernica, a parliamentary seat of Biscay Province, was utterly without any defenses and suffered accordingly.

"The destruction of the historic town of Guernica was planned by the Nazi Reichsminister Hermann Göring as a gift for Hitler's birthday, April 20…A brief initial bombing at 4:30 p.m. drove much of the population into an air-raid shelter. When Guernica's citizens emerged from these shelters to rescue the wounded, a second, longer wave of bombing began, trapping them in the town center, from which there was no escape. Low-flying planes strafed the streets with machine-gun fire. Those who had managed to survive were incinerated by the flames or asphyxiated by the lack of oxygen. Three hours of coordinated airstrikes leveled the city…The Führer was thrilled." *"A Life of Picasso: The Minotaur Years 1933-1943,"* John Richardson, pg. 135

To add insult to evil, the Nazis and Franco denied any responsibility for the bombing, lying that the Basques had destroyed their own town.

Drawn into the death-scene of Picasso's oil painting, Morgan felt the agonizing remnants of war: a gored horse; a skull superimposed over the horse whose tongue is replaced by three daggers; a bull formed from the horse's bent leg; a woman screaming, a dead child; a mutilated army officer; scattered swords and spears, a scorching sun; The Minotaur (body of a man, head of a bull); and The Harlequin (comedic character, sad clown).

The Minotaur perhaps symbolizes the painful despair at irrational wielding of military power; a Harlequin cries a diamond-shape tear for the victims of the vicious Nazi attack. Above in the painting, an oil lamp and a light bulb shine on Picasso's images below, creating a wake-up call to the world.

Pablo Picasso had been living in Paris for years when the bombing of Guernica took place. A German officer who saw a photo of Guernica asked: "Did you do that?" Picasso allegedly replied, "No, *you* did." Both Pablo and Lionel fought against the Nazis in their unique ways, and clearly it was a source of their mutual respect.

****

Picasso would ultimately join the Communist Party which didn't sit well with many Americans. In the following snippet of a 1953 radio interview (See Chapter 6) at the height of McCarthyism and the Red Scare in the United States,

Milton Mayer, reflecting that fear, pressed Lionel on the perceived rise in communism in France:

MM: But the multiplicities of political parties and the splintering of political parties, which is generally thought to have laid the groundwork for Nazism in Germany, does not appear to you as a sign to undermine France as a democracy? You have in France today the same rise of communism that we had in Germany in the first year or two of the 1930's.

LD: I wouldn't say there is any rise of Communism. In fact, there is a definite decline of Communism in France at the moment. There was a rise in Communism after the war, one due to economic conditions and two to the fact that the Communists did put up a rather good and effective fight against the Germans during the Resistance days. The Communists were the only organized party which was inside France and organized inside France when the liberation armies came, and that is why they had a terrific rise after liberation. Now I think they're on the decline.

MM: But the rise of Communism in Germany and certainly the French workers are very heavily communist if I am correctly informed. The rise of Communism in Germany gave rise in turn to the counter movement of Nazism. Isn't that possible also in France?

LD: I don't see it. I don't see it all because France would have only to call for a dictator or at least for a totalitarian man who presently exists in France as a political candidate. And so far, as I can see, the French have not voted very heavily for him, for this particular man or this particular group. The people still voted for democratic parties and not the French Communist Party.

****

"What do you think an artist is? He is a. political being, constantly aware of the heart breaking, passionate or delightful things that happen in the world, shaping himself completely in their image. Painting is not done to decorate apartments. It is an instrument of war. The meaning of life is to find your gift. The purpose of life is to give it away. Learn the rules like a pro, so you can break them like an artist."
Pablo Picasso

"Pablo Picasso was born in Malaga, Spain but came into his own amid the sleaze and bohemianism of Paris, the only city that could have matched his peerless imagination. Picasso spent the second world war in Paris, quietly working and supporting the Resistance. His defiance of the Nazi occupation made him even more inseparable from the story of this city."
"Pablo Picasso: "Spanish by birth, French at art," *The Guardian*, Jonathan Jones, February 20, 2015

Perhaps we can best understand how Picasso *created art as an instrument of war* through our earlier conversation about *Guernica* and by considering some of his paintings during the war years. On February 9, 1999, Michael Kimmelman wrote a *New York Times* Art Review of exhibits organized by the Fine Arts Museum of San Francisco and at the Guggenheim Museum in New York City, "Occupied Paris and the Politics of Picasso."

"When World War II began, Picasso chose to stick it out in his studio on the Rue des Grands-Augustins. He was not allowed to exhibit, but he managed to have paintings sold, some of which were bought by Germans, and he lived far more comfortably than most people did. Hitler had declared him to be a 'degenerate' artist, and according to one document, the German authorities ordered Picasso to report for a physical examination, a prelude to deportation to a labor camp. Although the document may have been a hoax, the evidence suggests that Picasso may well have believed it...how much can any of this— his Spanish Republicanism, his sentiments about the occupation, his Communist conversion—be detected in his art? This is the real subject of the present exhibition. It is a handsome, tendentious display of roughly 80 paintings, drawings, prints and sculptures (including "Man with a Lamb") from among the hundreds of works Picasso turned out during the war. A few motifs - skulls, candles, pitchers, food - dominate the many still life he painted. Food, of course, was scarce (although Picasso had his sources), and so was heat. One of the better pictures is a view from the inside of his studio through a window. In the foreground is a big radiator. The colors are brown and ice-blue and, as with his paintings of figures, the impression is of a solid mass, a kind of frozen sculptural form, not an open, airy space. 'But' Picasso went on, 'I have no doubt that the war is in these paintings I have done. Later on, perhaps the historians will find them and show that my style has changed under the war's influence.'" "*A Life of Picasso - The Minotaur Years 1933-1943*," John Richardson

Picasso was praised after the war as an influential Resistance artist. He was extolled for being actively involved with the French Resistance with his financial assistance though his principal contribution was in his creating art.

He also protected, hid and gave shelter to Jewish friends and artists being persecuted. Pablo saw to it that his writer friend, Max Jacob, was kept safe and protected. He took a strong anti-Fascist stance and felt that the French Communists were doing the most in the Resistance.

****

5. What's the Scoop?

Leo Genn, Lionel Durand c. 1948 Discuss 'Concert of Europe,' a peaceful system of diplomacy based on the balance of power among the strongest European countries from 1815 to 1914.

> *"No tears in the writer, no tears in the reader. No surprise in the writer, no surprise in the reader."*
> Robert Frost

> *"A human being is a part of the whole called by us "the universe," a part limited in time and space. He experiences himself, his thoughts and feelings as something separate from the rest...Our task must be to free ourselves from this prison by widening our circle of understanding and compassion to embrace all living creatures and the whole of nature in its beauty."* Albert Eins**Lionel Writes about Opera, 1960**

On April 18, 1947, a United Nations news clipping announced that Lionel was elected to represent the news media at the United Nations. Being chosen for this responsibility by his peers was a great compliment. He was well-regarded for his work as New York correspondent and foreign editor of the Paris newspaper *Le Paris-Presse.* He broadcast for Voice of America. By 1947, he had worked and lived in New York City for five years and his career was taking off. In 1951 he became editor of the international magazine *Ere Nouvelle* (The New Era) published in French and English.

****

Lionel reported on many international crises during the Cold War. On November 10, 1948, *The Circleville Herald* (Pickaway, Ohio), published Lionel's story *Paris Newspaper Insists Truman, Stalin Talk Set.* The Paris newspaper *Paris-Presse* writes, "Rumors persisted that President Truman would meet with Premier Stalin if the Berlin crisis was not settled by year's end." The newspaper cited White House denials, but there were wide rumors that the President had decided on such a meeting if the United Nations failed to achieve a settlement on the blockade issue in Berlin."

Another article by Lionel, writing as the *Paris-Presse* foreign editor, reported that "Information from an American source indicates the President plans to seek a new basis of American policy toward Russia". He added "that certain White House advisors frankly are urging a different attitude toward Moscow which could bring a new conciliation effort at the highest levels of the two governments."

Despite Lionel's initial scoop, Truman and Stalin never met in 1948.

****

"How can you govern a country which has 246 varieties of cheese?" Charles de Gaulle

"The Battle for France," an article written by Lionel for the *New Republic* (June 1951), gives an incisive analysis of France's June 17, 1951, legislative election. At 31 years of age, Lionel had his finger on the pulse of French post-war politics. Although based in New York, Lionel Spent a big part of his life in France at this tumultuous time. This 1951 election was crucial as France faced growing political instability. The

Fourth Republic had been established after the war, but political turmoil resulted in repeated calls for elections to address pressing issues such as colonial conflicts in Vietnam, Algeria, and Tunisia.

Lionel reported: "In just a few days, on June 17, the French people will go to the polls to elect a new Assembly to replace the one which, since November 1946, has made it hard for any coalition government to rule." One third of the legislative body was controlled by the Communist Party. To complicate matters, there were two thousand candidates and 14 national parties each of which would be allotted 10 minutes on live public radio for electoral propaganda. "Sharp differences among parties have forced eight successive cabinets out of existence in less than five years."

The campaign would be short, bitter and closely contested. Yet, Lionel stated that factions in the Assembly who fought each other over such issues as social security and Indochina "are now eager to stand together for another five-year ride." Further he wrote, "The Socialists and Christian Democrats stressed domestic issues such as economic growth by fortifying the value of the franc abroad and by building upon the country's comeback since the war and the occupation. The Communists parroted Soviet slogans for peace and against German rearmament and the war in Indochina. Some pundits claimed that de Gaulle, the great wartime leader, had lost touch with the people. But his opponents do not under-estimate his potential appeal as an honest man with complete integrity, little interest in money, and an uncompromising record as a staunch fighter for French prestige abroad. Can General de Gaulle succeed in convincing the large group of people who still see him as a potential dictator?"

Lionel wrote that the 1951 election might be "de Gaulle's last chance to play an important part in France's political life." De Gaulle founded the Rally of the French People (RPF) party in 1947. In the election, the RPF successfully gained some power to combat the Communist party by winning 120 seats in the National Assembly. The election resulted in a political realignment from center-left parties to center-right parties with the Democratic and Socialist Union of the Resistance (UDSR) receiving a majority. The election saw the emergence of General Charles de Gaulle, and, even though the Gaullists did not secure a parliamentary majority, the election laid a foundation for de Gaulle continuing as a key political figure in France.

By 1953 de Gaulle severed ties with the RPF, which disbanded in 1955. From 1955 to 1956, de Gaulle retired from public appearances to write his memoirs. At that time, Lionel correctly predicted that *le grand* Charles would return to power, and he did, becoming president of France on January 8, 1959.

****

"You can kill 10 of my men for every one of yours I kill, but even at those odds you will lose...Men and women, old and young, regardless of creeds or political parties, all Vietnamese must stand up to fight the French colonists to save the fatherland. Those who have rifles will use their rifles."
Viet Minh leader Ho Chi Minh warning French colonists in 1946

Starting in the early 1950's, Lionel reported on French colonial rule in Indochina. Ultimately, he became a seasoned journalist and expert on the subject, even writing about a French diplomat who wanted to negotiate a settlement directly with Ho Chi Minh. In his March 16, 1954, report, "New French Plan for Indochina," Lionel noted that the Viet Minh had already been fighting French Union Forces for eight years. "The near unanimous desire in France is to end the long, drawn-out war."

The Vietnamese would continue to resist outside foreign domination and colonization - first by France then by the United States - for the next two decades.

****

Lionel Durand, towering over Nikita Khrushchev in a 1957 informal press gaggle.

"If you live among wolves, you have to act like a wolf."
Nikita S. Khrushchev

Though it's debatable whether Khrushchev actually said this, it captures his tough confrontational and dramatic leadership style and the competitive nature of the Cold War. Khrushchev warned, *"When you are skinning your customers, you should leave some skin on to heal, so that you can skin them again."*

In 1957, Lionel was among the first reporters from the West to talk to Nikita S. Khrushchev (1894-1971), First Secretary of the Communist Party of the Soviet Union (1953-1964).

Lionel was covering the four-day and four-night celebration of Bolshevism's fortieth anniversary. Long-winded Nikita got things rolling with a three-hour speech to 17,000 Communists from 61 nations. He bragged that Communism had become a "mighty world system."

"His sputniks launched, and his rule secured, at least momentarily, Nikita S. Khrushchev was wheeling and dealing from strength, rattling rockets, and talking peace on Soviet terms."

"Khrushchev was the life of the party. He waltzed with a blonde and sang the Marsellaise at a Kremlin party of 3,000."

Lionel visited a Russian school in which Russian traditions and discipline were instilled in the students. In an English class, a 14-year-old girl asked Lionel in good English, "I study English at school. Do American girls of my age study Russian?" The electromagnetic shop was busy with boys and girls "turning out industrial tools with modern machinery."

"Did the teacher feel," Lionel inquired, "that it was more important to make children happy or to make them useful?"

The teacher replied with deep conviction: "How can they be happy if they are not useful?"

****

"The purpose of a writer is to keep civilization from destroying itself." Albert Camus

As a former French Resistance fighter, Lionel "knew most of the major figures of that heroic era, up to and including President de Gaulle." Lionel regularly interviewed de Gaulle at press conferences about the war and world and French politics. He also took the photograph of de Gaulle that was used as *Newsweek's* cover in its Feb 8, 1960, edition.

Unaware that these would become his last published pieces, Lionel contributed three stories for *Newsweek*, January 24, 1961: "The Periscope," p. 9-10; "On NATO," p. 26; "Belgium, The Showdown," p. 40.

A story by Lionel in "The Periscope" that week was: "*From Tunis*, Paris is ready to sign an agreement to turn its big navy base at Bizerte over to Tunisia much sooner than originally planned. This was in reward for Tunisian President Bourguiba's efforts to moderate the Algerian rebel demands and his backing of de Gaulle as the best man to end the Algerian war."

In the article, "On NATO," Lionel begins, "One hundred and ten miles behind the Iron Curtain lies a city that the West can neither defend nor give up. This is West Berlin, so often threatened by Communist siege that much of the world is tired of hearing about it. But by the time Caroline Kennedy is rolling Easter eggs on the White House lawn, a new Berlin crisis is virtually certain. What will the West do then?"

Lionel listed the players, "The British want to negotiate a new status for Berlin, and John Kennedy said he would agree if the Russians made concessions. Charles de Gaulle wants to maintain Western troops in Berlin even if by force. Germany's Chancellor Konrad Adenauer wants neither to concede anything nor to have a crisis. Such discord dramatizes a more basic problem facing Mr. Kennedy. At the heart of the problem is NATO."

Lionel further reported, "UN Secretary-General Paul-Henri Spaak says the (NATO) alliance must combat Russia's economic offensive in the underdeveloped world. The objection: NATO aid might smack of 'colonialism'. The NATO Supreme Commander in Europe, General Lauris Norstad, said 'NATO should acquire its own nuclear weapons. The objection: It might intensify the arms race.'"

In the article "Belgium, The Showdown," Lionel sets the disconcerting scene: "For 31 agonizing months, Belgium's dapper Premier Gaston Eyskens had wrestled with his country's problems. He had set the Congo free - only to see the Congo explode into anarchy and send thousands of hapless Belgians fleeing for their lives. He had appealed to the UN for help only to have Belgium branded as an aggressor, spurned by allies, and threatened by the Communist bloc. Then when Eyskens presented the bill for the Congo's loss to his humiliated people, half of them rose against him. Orderly little Belgium was rent with strikes that set Walloon against Fleming, Catholic against Protestant, Conservative against Socialist."

Eyskens was successful in making sure that Russia's attempt to label Belgium as an aggressor failed at the UN. "But the pressure had been too much. As he sat in Parliament his face grew pale and he had to be helped from the chamber. Sheer exhaustion, pronounced the doctor, as the plucky 55-year-old Premier of Belgium was carried home to bed."

A Final and More Personal Back Story: H.D. (Hilda Doolittle (1886–1961)

> *"My ancestry could be described as pure New England, where witches are burned, and we fought the Indians...I wanted to write poems by splashing ink from the pen all over my clothes to give me a feeling of freedom and indifference."* H.D.

There was an unusual and unexpected encounter between Lionel and the septuagenarian poet and writer Hilda Doolittle (H.D). During the last year of each of their lives, Lionel and Hilda impacted each other.

Born in Bethlehem, Pennsylvania, Hilda wrote award-winning poetry for five decades, friends with T.S. Eliot (1888-1965); William Butler Yeats (1865-1939); and Ezra Pound (1885-1972) who was Hilda's first love. To Ezra, Hilda was "Dryad" the wood spirit, the muse who inspired his early poetry.

Newsweek's Lionel Durand went to interview Hilda in April 1960 in Zurich, after Hilda's completing *"Bid Me to Live."* Then they met in New York City in May 1960 when she received the gold medal for poetry from the American Academy of Arts and Letters. Hilda described conversing with Lionel, a "Haitian," comparing him to 1960 gold medalist decathlon superstar, Rafer Johnson (1934–2020) whom Hilda referred to as a heroic, good-looking, muscular, shining God of Olympia. Hilda proclaimed, "Women are seeking, as one woman, fragments of the Eternal Lover." Lionel, handsome, 6'2", dark, radiating an intense charisma, listening deeply, became such a shining fragment for Hilda.

Here is a particularly revealing poem written by Hilda after meeting Lionel in which she voices her feelings for Lionel and offers him a lyrical complaint full of love.

Why did you come to trouble my decline?
I am old (I was old till you came)
the reddest rose unfolds
(which is ridiculous in this time, this place
unseemly, impossible even slightly scandalous),
the reddest rose unfolds.
H.D. From *Red Rose and a Beggar* (August 17–August 24, 1960)

6. A 1953 Conversation with Milton Mayer

Lionel Durand Voice of America c. 1949

American Archive of Public Broadcasting
Voices of Europe
Interview by Milton Mayer, American author, lecturer, and broadcaster; professor of Social Research from the University of Frankfurt. Interview recorded from Paris, January 1, 1953

Introduction: Mr. Durand has been a Frenchman living for 20 years in France although he was born in 1920 in Haiti. During the Second World War, he was a member of the intelligence group of the French Underground in Paris. Then he became New York correspondent and foreign editor of the Paris newspaper *Le Paris Presse*. He broadcast for Voice of America. In 1951, he became editor of the international magazine *Ere Nouvelle* (*The New Era*) published in French and English.

MM: Mr. Durand, how *decadent* is France?

LD: Well, I'd like you to qualify that a little more, Mr. Mayer. What do you mean by decadent?

MM: Well, let's start out with how decadent France is in terms of the American tourist view of France as a place where you can have the time of your life, and anything goes. Is France morally decadent?

LD: Well, I wouldn't agree with that view because for one thing I think there is an idea of Paris which American tourists have which unfortunately or fortunately we, Parisians, haven't been able to accept. By that I mean I have never seen people here selling filthy pictures to me or to any other Frenchman I know. I have never been to the *Follies Bergère* except when I was a young student and thought it was a thrill to go, but soon I found it very uninteresting and rather dull.

If you mean also that American tourists find that plumbing is not good or up to what it is in America, I don't think it is a very big thing to even argue about. Everyone knows American civilization is much younger and based on more material progress than it is in France. Certainly, we place less importance on Frigidaire's and plumbing than in America.

MM: That is, the civilization is younger, and the plumbing is accordingly younger and since America grew up in the age of plumbing, it puts in the French view undue emphasis on plumbing.

LD: Undue emphasis on plumbing, I agree.

MM: Now Mr. Durand, how decadent is France from another point of view, that is, from the point of view of our old friend Hitler, the Nazis, who took the point of view that France with its modern art, sybaritism, its self-indulgence represented everything that was not Aryan and non-heroic?

LD: I can understand this view, a view held not only by Hitler but by many others. People would say France has not developed after the war the kind of national trend and direction that would make it one of the big powers of the post-war period. I do think the reason France hasn't done that is that France is very eager to remain what it has been for so many centuries, that is *a crossroads for ideas and trends and not necessarily try to develop one idea and dictate it to the world.*

MM: I am thinking of Hitler and the Nazi view of the Maginot Line, for example, that France would put up some kind of defense but actually there was no defense. I think France would have put up a defense against Germany but actually there was no French strength, and there was no French heart, and there was no French Resistance, and the Nazi armies in fact did overrun France.

LD: It's true. They did overrun France because they were stronger than France in terms of armaments. I don't think you could say that of France today in terms of decadence because France has suffered so much from the war. You cannot compare material strength or such defenses that France could put up with anything that she is able to do actually.

MM: But you would argue, I take it, that none of the current history of France really reveals a basic decadence. That is, the fact that the economy is way up in the air, that the government falls every five minutes and what not. None of this represents the collapse of France and French civilization?

LD: No, I don't think that it does. I think you have a good point that governments fall every five minutes. It is quite a valid point. It is true that governments are not very stable in France. The reason for that is not that Frenchmen are unstable, but they have accepted the idea that you cannot have in only one political party all the tendencies and principles that a man can wish to have expressed in that one political party. That's why they have so many parties, and that is why you have a difficult task when you try to have a parliament representing so many parties to uphold only one government. These governments do fall but I find that broad policy, on foreign policy for instance, has remained the same for years. We have had only two foreign ministers since the liberation of France, and they have come from the same party, and they have applied the same program.

MM: But the multiplicities of political parties and the splintering of political parties, which is generally thought to have laid the groundwork for Nazism in Germany, does not appear to you as a sign to undermine France as a democracy?

LD: No, certainly not. I think that on some basic principles you'll find many Frenchmen of many different political parties agree completely.

MM: How then, Mr. Durand, would you contrast the French character or temperament with the German which did fall victim to this disintegrative process?

LD: Well, I think it's more than just a weakness of political parties in Germany which brought Hitler about. I think a lot had to do with the economic conditions in Germany, the fact that there was heavy unemployment, and that Hitler could easily make promises that he could keep in the beginning, as far as the great mass of disillusioned Germans were concerned.

MM: And yet you have in France today the same rise of Communism that we had in Germany in the first year or two of the 1930s.

LD: I wouldn't say there is any rise of Communism. In fact, I think there is a definite decline of Communism in France at the moment. There was a rise in communism after the war, one due to economic conditions and two to the fact that the Communists did put up a rather good and effective fight against the Germans during the Resistance days. They were the only organized party which was inside France and organized inside France when the liberation armies came, and that is why they had a terrific rise after liberation. Now I think they're on the decline.

MM: But the rise of Communism in Germany and certainly the French workers are very heavily communist if I am correctly informed. The rise of Communism in Germany gave rise in turn to the counter movement of Nazism. Isn't that possible also in France?

LD: I don't see it. I don't see it all because France would have only to call for a dictator or at least for a totalitarian candidate who exists in France. And so far, as I can see, the French have not voted very heavily for him, for this particular man or this particular group. The people still voted for democratic parties.

MM: Mr. Durand, before we leave Hitlerism, Nazism, and the contrast with the Germans, I am reminded of what appears to be the total absence of racial discrimination in France, which certainly sets France poles apart from the development of Nazism in Germany. It is this absence of racism, this total absence of racism in France at least as it appears, that has provided the real basis for the Nazis to call the French a decadent people.

LD: But I think that the Nazis have set as a general policy of attacking racial tolerance everywhere. I think they would attack any country which did not foster racial intolerance. What I would like to say is that when you say there is no racial discrimination in France, I think you are slightly wrong. There is a certain degree of prejudice in France against certain minorities and Negroes and Jews sometimes and Italians and Poles. But I don't think prejudice in France is based on their color or religion. It's based rather on the condition they are in intellectually or socially. In other words, if a good man happens to be a Negro in France, it does not make the slightest bit of difference.
MM: Why is that?

LD: I think it's that there has been a long tradition of liberalism, true liberalism in France for centuries.

MM: Mr. Durand, as the New York correspondent of the *Paris Presse* after the Second World War and as an American born in Haiti, as a Haitian, I assume that you were tempted to become an American citizen. Every American assumes that everybody is tempted to become an American. Were you? Did you resist the temptation? And why are you a Frenchman?

LD: Well, I was not tempted, I must say, to become an American. Not that I don't think it's a great country with vast possibilities and vast opportunities for people, but it just happens that I have lived in France most of my younger life, and I truly intended to become a Frenchman once again as soon as France would be free. And that's why I never thought of becoming an American.

MM: When we are talking about France and this allegation of decadence, I am reminded, of course, that it was here in France and in Paris that our own fathers, our own American founding fathers, such as Benjamin Franklin and Thomas Jefferson, were so wildly inspired with the idea of liberty.

LD: Yes, that's quite correct.

MM: Is the French idea of liberty in your view, as a last question, Mr. Durand, a stable one?

LD: Yes, I think it's quite stable and even so in everyday life. I think France is one of the very few countries where a man is free first to find himself and determine his own life and destiny, and that I think is basic freedom. He does not have to pretend to adhere to any system or any manner of speech or religion or anything like that in order to become a part of the "free group." He can be a free man if he is free himself and has found which way he wants to go and why.

MM: And is mankind in your view capable, competent to cope with this much freedom?

LD: Well, I don't think there can be too much freedom anywhere. As freedom develops, man will develop to adjust himself to that freedom. *Soon they will adjust themselves so much that freedom will have to adjust itself to man.*

MM: As a Frenchman, Mr. Durand, what would be your first suggestion if you were to make one to the Americans as to their conduct in their political, private, and public lives?
LD: That's a rather tough question I must say. I don't think I would advise Americans anything very specific except I would ask them to understand before they judge.

MM: Thank you very much, Mr. Durand.

7. Into the Eye of the Storm

"It is true, as Sartre once wrote, referring to French Army atrocities in Algeria, that the real tragedy in our time is that any of us can be interchangeably victim or torturer." Gore Vidal

"Lionel Durand was tear-gassed in Algeria, while covering riots that had erupted in the Casbah. He had gone there to interview Moslem leaders. Among his last stories were 'Algeria - You-You-You-You'' and 'Into the Eye of the Storm.' - Lionel Durand, who for two years was Newsweek's Paris bureau chief, had lived life to the hilt."
Epitaph - A Reporter, *Newsweek's* account of Lionel Durand's death (see Appendix 4)

"Perhaps the whole root of our trouble, the human trouble, is that we will sacrifice all the beauty of our lives, will imprison ourselves in totems, taboos, crosses, blood nations, in order to deny the fact of death, which is the only fact we have. It seems to me that one ought to rejoice in the fact of death - ought to decide, indeed, to earn one's death by confronting with passion the conundrum of life. One is responsible to life: it is the small beacon in that terrifying darkness from which we come and to which we shall return. One must negotiate this passage as nobly as possible, for the sake of those who are coming after us."
James Baldwin

Lionel died as a young war correspondent while covering the Algerian War. Wading into a violent demonstration in the Casbah, a tear-gas bomb exploded at his feet. He never fully recovered from his injuries. In June 1962, the Overseas Press Club's newsletter the *Bulletin* announced that, in a formal ceremony on the 17th anniversary of D-Day, that Lionel's name had been added to the OPC Memorial Room Honor Roll Roster, which honors newsmen killed in the performance of their journalistic duties, showing, with Lionel Durand added, a total of 93 names. A photo that accompanies the story shows Lionel Durand's name prominently displayed on the Honor Roll wall. (See Appendix 2)

He was only 40 years old.

****

Like most professions, journalists often use short, insider terms and phrases to capture the essence of their craft. One such term describing their published writing is "stuff." To tell a journalist that you "like their stuff" is high praise indeed. In keeping with that honored tradition, we have decided to cover Lionel's final journalistic work - covering the War for Independence in Algeria - by giving him his own voice back by recovering and presenting his own last dispatches amidst the violence and killings. His tragic death was directly tied to injuries he sustained while "getting the story." What better way to cover the last month of his life than to present what he, and his fellow combat journalists were cabling to their publishers in real time - "their stuff."

> *"300 ARE WOUNDED; Europeans Retaliate for Algerian Acts of Terrorism; TROOPS IN ALGIERS KILL 61 IN RIOTING" December* 12, 1960, The *New York Times*

"ARMY OPENS FIRE IN ALGIERS AGAIN; TOLL RISES TO 90 IN ALGIERS CLASH"—December 13, 1960, The *New York Times*

Lionel provided firsthand, on the scene reporting on Charles de Gaulle's historic visit to Algeria in December 1960:

"At a crowded movie theater in the Algerian port of Mostaganem, the chattering sounds from the screen were harshly interrupted by a sudden blast one night last week. An Algerian rebel bomb had gone off, injuring 25 people.

This was the area that the French Army calls 'pacified.' Yet the bloodshed went on, and for at least the beginning of 1961, it would go on and on...

To stop it, Charles de Gaulle flies across the Mediterranean this week to put all his tremendous authority behind a new effort at settlement. His step-by-step plan for 1961: To declare a unilateral truce, set up an autonomous Algerian administration, win popular backing in a France-wide referendum, and then allow the Algerian people to vote on their own future. His hope is that the Algerian people will want to stay linked with France.

Can he pull it off?

One element in de Gaulle's favor is that the French Army has already achieved substantial military success. By its own claims, at least, it has sealed off the bulk of the FLN behind the Tunisian and Moroccan borders and reduced the active rebels to scattered bands totaling about 6,000 men. And, in economic development, by the end of 1961, the $11 billion 'Constantine Plan' will have created about 600 new corporations and about 150,000 new jobs.

Diehards: Yet it is this very progress that fills Algeria's 1.2 million Europeans and the 500,000-man French Army with a determination not to surrender hard-won gains. The *colons* (European Settlers) freely predict 'a blood bath' and even 'another Budapest' if de Gaulle tries to create his 'Algerian Algeria.' And many conservative politicians and army officers back them up, 'I don't belong to a nation of quitters and cowards,' one captain declared. 'I have nothing to lose by fighting on, even against other Frenchmen.' But the FLN also vows to fight on."
Europe-The Squeeze, December 12, 1960, *Newsweek*

****

Over the coming days, Lionel reported on de Gaulle's historic visit to Algeria:

"It was a season of raw winds and long darkness. And in the darkest time of the year, from Paris south across the Mediterranean, some felt a strange sense of foreboding, a smell of danger and violence in the air. Almost inevitably, violence exploded in tormented Algeria.

There, mobs of Europeans and Moslems clashed in pitched battles with French troops and police. There in the tense pauses between the daily riots, the smell of tear-gas and smoke lay like a mist over the rubble littered streets. There, the conflicts swirled around a tall, lonely 70-year-old man, who was endowed with a quality of personal grandeur and sheer courage that could change the tides of history.

General Charles de Gaulle had flown to Algeria because he had decided that there was only one way to end the civil war that had drained both France and North Africa. Six years of savage fighting had proved to his mind and to many Western officials that the solution lay neither in eternal French rule nor in giving way to the Communist-backed FLN rebels. Instead, he was determined to rally the silent, frightened Moslem masses into voting freely on their own government and on their own future.

Given such a choice, he was convinced that most Algerians would choose to build an 'Algerian Algeria' closely bound to France. But Algeria's 1.2 million Europeans, and many soldiers there were determined that France should rule Algeria forever. To impose his solution on the Moslems and Europeans alike with the full backing of the Western Allies, de Gaulle flew into the eye of the storm."

After being severely injured by a tear gas bomb in the tumult on the first day of the unrest, December 10, 1960, Lionel continued to cable reports from Algeria in the following days.

"On the scene, *Newsweek's* Lionel Durand cabled this account:

"As de Gaulle's motorcade entered the square, tough, steel helmeted Gards Mobiles pushed the shouting Europeans back. Inside the city hall, de Gaulle told local officials: 'Algeria is being transformed through huge and very cruel trials...There must be peace.'

Defiance: As the shouting outside grew, de Gaulle shrugged. 'Noise, shouts—that signifies nothing,' he snapped. 'Algeria's future is entirely in Algeria's hands, not in France's.' Then he turned and went to the door. 'I know that if I go out, they (the crowd) will start yapping all the more,' he told the mayor. 'But I am going out!'

With that, de Gaulle stepped out of the city hall. Ignoring the Europeans, who were crying 'traitor!' the general walked over to a gathering of Moslems. Brushing aside his bodyguards, he strode in among them. The excited Moslems clasped de Gaulle's hands and kissed them. Suddenly, there was a new cry, this time from the Moslems 'Vive de Gaulle!' 'Algérie Algérienne.'

A French officer standing next to me said: 'That de Gaulle! He's got more guts than this entire mob put together.'

As de Gaulle continued from town to town, he was hailed by thousands of Moslems. De Gaulle had unquestionably won the first round. But other rounds remained. And in the sprawling, half-modern, half-slum city of Algiers, it was a different story."

"Despite government warnings of reprisal, a general strike virtually paralyzed all commerce and transport." **Into the Eye of the Storm** December 19, 1960, *Newsweek*

****

Though injured, Lionel proceeded with his days of unrelenting and intense reporting:

"The official death toll for the week of rioting was 127. Statistically, that was nothing, not in Algeria, where the war has taken an average weekly toll of 500 for six years. But these were no unknown rebels killed in some obscure mountain gully. These were Arab schoolboys and shopkeepers shot down before the eyes of a watching world.

The world had seen Charles de Gaulle fly to Algeria to mobilize support for his program of Algerian self-government. It had seen the European colons start rioting against him. Then something happened that never had happened before. The Moslems marched through the streets shouting 'Algérie Algérienne.' This was de Gaulle's own slogan, but the Casbah had awakened and spoken, not for France but for the FLN rebels."

From Algiers, where he was recovering from the effects of tear gassing, *Newsweek's* Lionel Durand cabled: 'Go in, if you want,' the captain told me, 'But, you're crazy to want to.'"

"The captain was one of 11,000 beret-topped paratroopers who manned the barbed-wire barricades cutting off every entrance to the Casbah. I walked past the troops through a narrow passageway leading into what is a city within a city, a mountaintop maze of Moslem slums. On the square some 2,000 Moslems shouted 'Algérie Algérienne.' A young student actually appeared to be frothing at the mouth as he waved a dagger in his left hand and the green and white FLN flag in his right. A man approached me: 'You want an exclusive interview on how I killed twelve Frenchmen?' From hundreds of white-robed women came the piercing Arab war cry chant: 'You-you-you-you.' Sealed off within their citadel, the Moslems could not vent their hatred on the French. So, they turned against the Jews who lived in the Casbah. Twice within 24 hours, they sacked the synagogue that Napoleon III had built for Algiers Jewry a century ago. The sacred Torah lay torn in shreds on the sidewalk. Shots rang out as the mob smashed Jewish store windows, and hundreds of Jews fled to seek protection from the French.

French forces soon moved into the Casbah to restore a semblance of order. But the shouting began again as soon as the soldiers passed. Later, when a Moslem crowd filed out of the Casbah to bury their dead in the nearby cemetery of El Kettar, the women suddenly tore off their veils, unfurled their FLN flags, and began clawing their faces in grief. At their renewed cries, the men began shouting for the FLN leader: 'Ferhat Abbas to power.' And back in the Casbah market, where the demonstrations continued day after day, one Moslem told me: 'This is our vote. We are all for the FLN and Moslem Algeria. Write that.'

It was Charles de Gaulle who first had called on the long silent Moslem masses to 'fulfill your responsibilities' and 'make your influence felt.' His hope was that the Moslems would work with him for his goal of an autonomous Algeria, closely bound to France. But the FLN moved in swiftly. At a secret meeting within the Casbah, a dozen top FLN leaders decided to mobilize the Moslems for a show of strength.

It was these men who handed out the FLN flags and steered the demonstrators into the streets. But the one thing they needed to weld the crowd together was violence from the *colons*, and the *colons* provided that. As the French Army faced the Moslems, I heard the European crowd shouting: 'Kill them! Kill them!' The killings that followed - out of the 127 officially announced as dead, all but eight were Moslems - may well have destroyed all of de Gaulle's hopes of conciliation between the two factions. Six years of war and suffering have taught nothing to the hotheads on both sides."

Break Their Backs

"What happens next in Algeria depends on one man - de Gaulle. As the lofty French President flew home to

Paris last week, calling an emergency Cabinet meeting and ordering his police to crack down on the extremists of both sides." *Newsweek's* bureau reported, 'There is only one policy,' a grim-faced Charles de Gaulle declared to the tensely silent crowd that braved the cold and snow flurries to greet his homecoming blue and silver Caravelle jet. 'It must be followed because it is the good one.'"

"That policy was the same one that de Gaulle had decided on before his ill-fated trip: A nationwide referendum on Jan. 8 to give him authority to dictate a self-governing 'Algerian Algeria.' De Gaulle was virtually certain to win his plebiscite by a huge majority (as high as 80 per cent)." **Algeria-you-you-you-you,** December 26, 1960, *Newsweek*

****

Algerian eyewitnesses describe the events of December 1960 in Algeria

The massive demonstrations in December 1960 were vividly captured in the 2020 documentary, *Only One Hero, the People* where eyewitnesses to the events spoke of their losses and trauma as well as their joy and healing. The film, directed by Mathieu Rigouste, documents the people's uprising against French rule while under continual French military repression. It was the Algerian working classes, *sometimes with women and children on the front line,* leaving their shantytowns in their segregated neighborhoods, that defied French colonial rule. This was the crucial turning point in the Algerian war with the people taking their rebellion to the streets for nearly three weeks. The film includes archival clips of the massive outpouring and reveals the bravery and unity of individual people, who are described in the film as the true *heroes* of this vital history.

The director Mathieu Rigouste explains: "It was the popular classes who took the revolution in hand, took it to the cities, marching over the streets and into the forbidden neighborhoods." The famous slogan referring to the uprising was *Only One Hero, the People.*

Only One Hero, the People

"We were living in a form of apartheid. We were completely isolated." Djamila Amran, inhabitant of Algiers in 1960

"Look at the conditions people lived in. I'll skip over the barefoot details. Any form of uprising, any form of resistance, any form of insurrection had to be destroyed brutally, deeply and in a durable way. It targeted not only the insurgents, but it was also aimed at the people." Daho Djerbal, Algerian historian

"I have some vague but vivid memories. I was told that our village had been decimated. The French army picked up all the men. They loaded them on trucks and took them a few miles from the village. They killed all of them, except one." Messaouda Chaban, inhabitant of Algiers in 1960

"My uncle Ali was arrested in 1957, during the Battle of Algiers. He suffered 40 days of torture, and he died

under torture. We read about it in the papers, meaning the military didn't have the decency to notify the family of his death." Fadmila Amrane, niece of lawyer, Ali Boum

"*I was fortunate to have survived through this whole period, from my childhood, from the age of 10 in a revolutionary family. Before December 1960, I had been arrested and tortured four times… So, when December 1960 came, it was a joy, it was freedom! We finally are going to express ourselves. We finally are going to cry out for freedom.*" Hocine Belkacemi, FLN militant in Algiers in 1960

"*I lived and I was born at the foot of the prison where the guillotine was. You see and hear neighbors calling out to the others,* **Today, Abdel Zaghahat will be executed***. The women were ululating, high-pitched piercing sounds of tears and screaming* (youyous). *We saw our dads burst into tears. I lived these executions in my very flesh. I will carry this trauma for the rest of my life. But despite all the repression and all the military force, the resistance hasn't stopped for one day… We were spellbound and it lasted eight days and eight nights in December of 1960. We slept neither day nor night. In the morning, we demonstrated, and in the evening we all met up with our families. No one was keeping an eye out.*" Lounes Ait Aouda, demonstrator at the Casbah of Algiers, December 1960

Starting in 1959, my family was decimated. My brother Mohammad was killed. My father was killed. He was 54 years old when first arrested. There was fierce

repression...The French army dumped victims' bodies out in the open lot or barely buried in a dump next to the military base. From 1960, we were arrested with my mother, taken as hostages. We were sequestered for eight months. We were tortured very cruelly. I was being tortured in front of my mother and vice-versa, and when my father was killed, his remains were strapped to the hood of a military vehicle. He was transported to the town, and we couldn't recover his body." Aissan Nedjari was one of the demonstrators in 1960.

"The demonstrations of December 1960 should be treated not as an exception, but as an extraordinary illustration of the popular and spontaneous dynamics that animated the FLN and the people-based revolution...We cannot understand the history of the Algerian Revolution without understanding the astuteness, courage, and passion with which ordinary Algerians acted to liberate themselves on, before and after December 11." (Cf. *The Journal of North African Studies*, "The December 1960 Demonstrations in Algeria: Spontaneity and Organization of Mass Action," Nadia Sariahmed Belhadj, 2022)

Women took a prominent role in the demonstrations; they would sing at the barricades "France you killed all the young men. When they are no more, the women will take on the sacred combat." France had robbed these women of their loved ones, and they sent a clear message that they would continue the fight for freedom. During demonstrations, women made high-pitched, ululating, trilling sounds, highly emotional vocal expressions called *youyous*. New York City

Psychoanalyst in Paris and Algiers, Karima Kazali states that *"youyous are a kind of portage that's going to bring rhythmicity, an impulse and a rhythm that will pass through other bodies. It's about making one's own body a part of the revolt."*

Collective Catharsis

Dancing as portrayed in the film became a collective catharsis for the atrocities suffered by Algerians and offers an ecstatic release from the pain of subjugation inflicted by the French. Saida Nait Bouda, an Algerian choreographer, explains what Algerian traditional dance is about.

> *"One day I saw some traditional dances, and I understood what a real traditional dance is, and at that point I went even more towards trance rituals, ecstatic rituals, and contrary to what one might imagine in trance rituals, people don't get up and dance. They dance because they can't help it. So, there's already an inner tension that is compelling you to get up; there's an explosion...It's all about community art."*

Dancing and music provide a communal atmosphere encouraging expressions of pain and suffering as well as joy and bliss in a non-verbal, visceral way to release pent up emotions from trauma. While the Algerian people did achieve liberation and the right to self-determination, they would remain individually and collectively scarred. Karima Lazali explains, *"The body of the colonized and colonial violence is that the colonized is someone who is excluded from humanity. That's how they are being treated politically, and so it is a body that is very rigid, highly stressed and finally, it can result in a*

133

permanent explosion. For them liberation in this colonial context can only be achieved by releasing the vital energies in the body and music and dance are the best way to reclaim those energies that are encrusted in the body, that are prohibited from movement, to release them, and reconnecting them through the function of the dance and trance in the traditional manner."

****

Human rights abuses by French Soldiers in Algeria

Patrick Rotman made a four-hour 2002 documentary, *"The Intimate Enemy, Violence in the Algerian war,"* a "collective questioning" of human nature. Rotman interviewed dozens of French veterans who admitted to having seen or practiced torture, rape, and summary executions.

> "Men in their 60s - including Jean Faure, the vice president of the French Senate - wept openly as they recounted secrets they had kept their whole adult lives. While Rotman's witnesses venture explanations - racism, peer pressure, the abuse of alcohol, anger, and the desire for revenge - the most disturbing explanation was a former soldier's mention of 'a form of pleasure' doing whatever you want to a body, fulfilling your most perverse and deep desires."
> *The Irish Times*, "Breaking the Silence," Lara Merton, March 16, 2002

French WWII Resistance Fighters Aligned with the Algerian FLN

Martin Evans, in *History Today* July 1991, interviewed Frenchmen who actually helped the Algerian FLN in direct opposition to the French military: "Across the oral testimonies we found that a sense of the Second World War was central in explaining their motivations for resistance to the Algerian war. In 1954, there were two hundred thousand Algerians living in France. Of the French people actively involved with the FLN, the most famous were those associated with the Jeanson network which was intellectually associated with Jean-Paul Sartre. During the late 1940s and early 1950s, Jeanson had visited Algeria twice. Shocked by colonialism, he contacted Algerian nationalists and, returning to France, he wrote a number of articles warning of the explosive situation."

Aline Charby, whom Martin Evans interviewed, joined the Jeanson network as she "saw the Algerian struggle against colonialism in terms of the French Resistance. The colonial mentality was a continuation of collaboration and to be done away with."

"Pierre Deeschemacker was a Roman Catholic priest who was sent to Algeria in 1955. He told Evans in his interview: 'In the evening, I saw the body of an Algerian, which had been left on the street by the French army. This immediately reminded me of the Occupation, even if I had not seen such atrocities myself. I was deeply shocked to see that the body was still there four or five hours after the fighting. The normal human reaction would have been to take the body away. It was obvious that it had been left there to inspire fear and terror in the Algerian population.'"

Yet French resistance to the Algerian War was limited. Martin Evans concludes:

"We are talking about 1,000 people, 4,000 at most. Why? If the connection between the Second World War resistance and the resistance to colonialism was so obvious for them, why was it not for many more people? The answers to these questions involve consideration of the language of the majority and the strength of other influences such as colonialism, racism, patriotism, nationalism, and the belief in the civilizing mission of France."

****

The Immediate Impact: The France/Algeria Referendum Vote

In what would be one of his very last stories before he died, Lionel reported on the Referendum Vote both in France and in Algeria.

"To win the support he wanted (for a referendum on Algerian self-determination on January 8, 1961), de Gaulle's government distributed 6 million copies of a magazine called *France Referendum* and 700,000 records of his speeches. More importantly, it ordered the army to run the referendum in Algeria and crush FLN demands for a boycott.

Army loudspeakers blared through hillside villages with the simple instruction: Vote 'Oui.' The army trucked Moslems to the polls or went after them with 200 jeep-mounted polling stations. And scattered demonstrations favoring the FLN rebels were answered with gunfire.

In the fabled old town of Sidi-bel-Abbes, headquarters of the Foreign Legion, three Moslems were shot to death while trying to erect FLN flags on public buildings. To the east, a crowd of 200 Moslems smashed store windows as they rampaged through Tiaret. Troops opened fire, leaving five dead and 30 wounded. Total casualties during the three-day voting steadily climbed toward 100.

But though the FLN enforced a substantial boycott in the big cities, about 60 per cent of all eligible voters went to the polls. One woman, asked why she was voting, answered: 'I don't know. Soldiers told me to.' But a Moslem chief outside Bone declared: 'We're all voting yes, because if *Bouya* (Father) de Gaulle goes, the war will drag on for another twenty years.'

The most fundamental opposition, of course, comes from the FLN itself. The rebels now have the full support of the Soviet bloc, which has recently shipped in 2,500 tons of arms, plus the firm backing of many influential Afro-Asian leaders. 'This year will be a good one,' FLN leader Ferhat Abbas said last week. 'We will be in Algiers by the end of 1961.'

Early this week, when the votes were counted, de Gaulle won 75 percent of the ballots cast in France and 65 per cent in Algeria. But many abstentions left him with only 54 per cent of all voters. It was much less than the 'massive' mandate he had asked; his narrow victory could scarcely provide more than the beginning of a solution."

Stormy Algeria - Only a Start

Lionel Durand, *Newsweek* January 16, 1961.

8. Family Memories

"It is in the roots, not the branches, that a tree's greatest strength lies. If you know where you are from, it is harder for people to stop you from where you are going. A tree's beauty lies in its branches, but its strength lies in its roots."
Matshona Dhilwayo, Canadian-based philosopher and author

In 2020, Morgan received Facebook messages from Lionel Changeur (born 1972) and Jérémy Changeur (born 1977). They are the sons of Lionel's daughter and Morgan's sister, Barbara (July 16, 1952-December 10, 2010). They said that they did not know a lot about their grandfather. Lionel Changeur was named after him and would google his grandpa's name from time to time. Voilà! On November 28, 2020, to Lionel's surprise, the *Haitian Times* article where Morgan discusses finding his father, popped up. (see Appendix 5)

"We just discovered that our mummy Barbara had a brother - you!"

Barbara in 2009, Vendée Region, France

So, with enthused expectation, Morgan and his nephews gathered over the internet on Zoom, sharing about themselves, their own families, and their mother Barbara and grandmother, Irène Lipsz of New York City (October 21, 1924-June 9, 2022). They were joined by Lionel's wife,

Aurélie, and their daughters Noémie and Charlie. Jérémy was joined by his partner Chiara and their two young daughters, Alessia and Elisa.

Lionel, a journalist, related that he walks modestly "in Lionel Durand's footsteps, sometimes with a heavy burden on my shoulders. He was such a splendid example of the inaccessible model."

Jérémy and Lionel both expressed their abiding love for their mother Barbara who, unfortunately, like her father, suffered heart problems and hypertension and had passed away in 2010. Barbara had married twice, first with their father, François Changeur, and then with Léon Leroy.

"What do you think an artist is? He is a. political being, constantly aware of the heart breaking, passionate or delightful things that happen in the world, shaping himself completely in their image. Painting is not done to decorate apartments. It is an instrument of war. The meaning of life is to find your gift. The purpose of life is to give it away. Learn the rules like a pro, so you can break them like an artist."
Pablo Picasso

****

Pascale, Simone, and Martine (Left to Right)

The genesis of the Durand family reunion began with Simone Staco Rivière, Morgan's lovely cousin, who was the first close relative he found and who, with her daughters Pascale and Martine, along with her son-in-law Eduard, first introduced us to Lionel Durand.

Here is the story of how John and Morgan ultimately found Morgan's Haitian family through the use of Morgan's DNA.

DNA test results revealed that Morgan's father's heritage was largely from sub-Saharan Africa and that he was Black. Because the distant matches coming up were primarily from Haiti, we also knew that Morgan's father was most likely Haitian.

It would take us years after we started the DNA search before John finally discovered a close genetic match on Morgan's father's side, a second cousin, Simone Rivière. With such a close DNA match, John would finally be able to figure out who Morgan's father was.

On the first anniversary of that discovery, John recounted for Morgan the happy-ending story of his DNA detective work. "Today (January 5, 2020) we celebrate the Feast of the Epiphany. One year ago today, I got up very early, while it was still dark, put on a suit and tie (so as to look respectable and not scare your second cousin, Simone) and drove out to her house in the city."

"The afternoon before, I had called Simone at her home, and attempted to tell her about you and how you were adopted as a little boy, and never knew your father or who he even was until now with the DNA revealing that you were Haitian and her second cousin."

"Confused, Simone passed the phone over to one of her daughters, Pascale, whose family she lived with. Pascale got on the phone, listened respectfully for a few minutes before, assuming I was some sort of a con artist, politely, yet firmly, told me that they were not interested and hung up."

"Thus, I made my decision to go to their home early the next day and attempt to talk to Simone in person. Armed with pictures of you as a boy and your DNA test results, I knocked on her door. Just as I had hoped, Simone was an early riser, and I got to speak to her directly while everyone else in the house was still sleeping. I told her your story and hearing my pleas and seeing your pictures as a boy and recognizing a family resemblance, she gave me the names of her four grandparents and the contact information of her other son-in-law, Eduard, the family's historian. Eduard is the husband of Simone's second daughter, Martine."

"Simone told me: Morgan looks like a member of our family. But promise me you will not contact Eduard until late this afternoon as he was up all night and needs his sleep."

"True to my word and stopping only to go to Mass, and to beseech the heavens for assistance, I reviewed the names of all four of Simone's grandparents and worked on the family tree in my car, camping out in front of Martine's house— waiting. Finally, Martine and Eduard emerged with their son in the late afternoon, and we at last made contact."

"They were so incredibly nice and kind to me, sharing with me additional genealogical information that finally, finally, led us, in a little more than a week, to discovering that Lionel Durand was your dad! After all these years of searching, he was finally found! You, Morgan, were home! It truly was the Feast of the Epiphany."

Simone, Morgan's newfound second cousin, is the granddaughter of Lamercie Durand (1873–1945), who was Lionel Durand's aunt, his dad's sister. By discovering all the siblings of Simone's grandmother Lamercie, we knew that one of them would be Morgan's grandparent.

At 6:55 a.m., January 15, 2019, auspiciously Dr. Martin Luther King Jr. Day, John texted Morgan: "MORGAN CALL ME. Very important!! We found your dad!!!!!"

Lamercie Durand (1873-1945) sister of Lionel Durand's father, Louis Durand

Simone, Martine and Pascal and their family celebrated the discovery. Just as they would when they learned the news of Morgan meeting his nephews, Lionel and Jérémy Changeur, and cousin, Chantal Larouche. Martine wrote:

"Dear cousin. What terrific news! Chantal is indeed our cousin. Her grandfather Camille, yours Louis Durand and Lamercie, my great grandmother, were siblings. Finding your nephews is a beautiful Christmas present. I am so happy Chantal got in touch with you. And that our family just got bigger. We still hope to meet you soon. Warm hugs from your family here in New York!"

Chantal Laroche and Son, Christopher Freedom Laroche

Lionel Changeur had sent the link of the *Haitian Times* article (see Appendix 6) to Chantal who responded, "Everyone in the family is so happy to meet a new relative. We are all excited. This is a pleasure to have all the information possible to get closer to our dear cousin, Morgan. I live in Cap-Haïtien, Haiti. My grandfather was Camille Durand, brother of Lamercie Durand and of Louis Durand, Lionel's papa, your grandpa. Hope to hear from you soon." Bisous

Chantal's son, Christopher "Freedom" Laroche (born December 31, 1984) is an accomplished singer and composer, whose music videos are available on YouTube. In the early 2000s, after being assaulted by more than a dozen men, Christopher was lying in a bed in a Toronto hospital, going in and out of a coma, begging God to help him recover and promising to do something special for Haiti should he survive. "The only thing I remembered was that I was Haitian; I did not remember my name. I did not remember anything. At that point, I felt like my love for Haiti became magic." Through Chris' music and his advocacy for Haiti and for the world's most vulnerable children, he continues to keep his promise to do something special for Haiti.

In 2016 in response to hurricane Matthew in Haiti and as a protest against human trafficking, Christopher wrote the song "Dream a World." The song is a story of going home, embracing family, a mission of love and caring for Haiti and children worldwide. Chantal: "I cannot be more grateful for my son's music. Singing about Haiti is the pride of all Haitians."

Lyrics of 2016 "Dream a World" (CNN edition) by Freedom on Youtube Video

(Verse)

Dream a world where everything's gold

So money means nothing

And you can't sell your soul

I dream a world where we all grow

Learn from our past and let things go

Nobody's homeless and nobody's cold

Not desperate for nothing so nobody stole

I dream a world that we can be proud of

But that can't exist if we forget about love

(Chorus)

Ooooooooouuuuuu

Ooooooooouuuuuu

Just march along

Ooooooooouuuuuu

Ooooooooouuuuuu

Just march along

(Verse)

Dream a world where everything's gold

So money means nothing

And you can't sell your soul

I dream a world where we all grow

Learn from our past and let things go

Everyone's healthy and nobody's stressed

No reason for sadness so none of it's left

(Bridge)

I dream a world that's not far away

And I dream a world

For you I have prayed

(Chorus)

I dream a world
Ooooooooouuuuuu
Ooooooooouuuuuu
I dream a world
Ooooooooouuuuuu
Ooooooooouuuuuu
I dream a world

****

Christopher clarifies his meaning of the lyric "where money is nothing and you can't sell your soul" in a CNN interview:

In the context of human trafficking, we were born in a country, Haiti, that is less fortunate. It's one of the most beautiful places in the world but it is also one of the poorest countries in the world. I wrote this song because I feel children should have the right to have a dream. I feel all around the world many children are able to become successful adults because they have the resources they need to make their dreams come true. In my *ideal Haitian world, I see a world where we don't place as much importance on money, where seeing the positive potential of the people back in Haiti, together with the Diaspora, would help create the conditions where Haitian children could enjoy the freedom of available resources and civil peace to live their cherished longings.*

Through Chantal, Morgan was able to email Chris, and we learned more about Chris's life and his artistic-activist invitation to love Haiti, love Haitians, love all, and organize to protect vulnerable children. Chris emailed: "Family, what a pleasure!!!! Would be happy to answer any questions, my brother Morgan. It is a pleasure to connect with you. I am honored that your friends were so moved by "Dream A World"; I will go deeper into the story and run it by for you…It's pretty deep. Blessings to you."

The memory of Lionel Durand and his own love for Haiti and human rights, and artistic, political, and religious freedom lives on in the musical artist and activist Christopher Freedom Larouche, a proud descendant of Lionel Durand.

****

Chantal and Josiane in Haiti

Lionel had two siblings: sister Andrée and brother René. In December 2020, Morgan was thrilled to receive a warm email from his cousin, Josiane Stark, Andrée's daughter and Lionel's niece.

"Hello, Morgan. I feel so grateful to have another cousin, and I feel that you are already part of our family. I didn't have the happiness to know your father Lionel who was my mother Andrée's brother, my uncle. When Lionel, your dad, passed away, my mother told me that I was only five months old. Now I am sixty-five. I have two older brothers, your cousins, Joel and Alain, sons of Andrée. Joel unfortunately passed away just four months ago at the age of seventy-seven years old. Joel was a dear person; we miss him a lot. He has a son, Jean Luc, who is my nephew and my godchild. He has three children. My other brother Alain is so dear to me as well. He is alive and healthy; his wife's name is Michelle."

"You know about Micheline, our dear cousin (Lionel's niece) who lives in France. She is happy to share precious souvenirs of Uncle Lionel with you. I would love to communicate with you. Chantal, Sébastien, Jérémy, and Lionel are so pleased to know about your existence. Micheline and I already feel very close to you. God bless you too, and I am in a hurry to have the confirmation that you got my message. A big hug d'eau, my dear cousin. From Josiane"

****

Hello from Italy

Sébastien Stark, Josiane's son, with wife Rowan

Josiane's son, Sébastien Stark, contacted Morgan in 2020 via Facebook messages. "Dear Morgan, forgive me for the impromptu message as we have not met before. It appears that we are related. My apologies for the strange claim. This borders on absurdity, but I just received the most incredible article from my mother Josiane who's based in Haiti. She sends me daily online articles, and I must admit that a lot of them do go unnoticed. The *Haitian Times* article wasn't one of them! I read your amazing story about your father, Lionel Durand, my great uncle! I was born and raised in Haiti and have been living in Dubai for the past 10 years with my wife and three-year-old daughter. My mother Josiane Saurel was born to Luc Saurel and Andrée Durand, your father's sister. Andrée fled France to Haiti during the war. Sadly, she was murdered in 1992. My sincerest apologies if this message comes across as strange, and you would be right to think of it as such, but I was really compelled to reach out. My mother, Josiane, found your writing lovely, and was hoping I could help her get a close up of the picture featured in the article. There are quite a few interesting chapters in our family history that I would love to share with you if you are interested. I am happy to write, and please know that I am not expecting to hear back from you, but secretly hoping that this message puts a smile on your face and that we are able to connect for the sake of at least helping you connect more dots! Have a wonderful weekend and in case I never hear back from you, I am glad to know that you were able to find some of those roots."

Sébastien did hear back from Morgan and the two have spoken on the telephone and have gotten to know each other as well as his wife, Rowan, and two enchanting daughters, Rafaelle and Romy through WhatsApp, email, and Facebook.

****

Micheline celebrating her 80th birthday

Morgan first connected with his cousin, Micheline Durand (born 1941), Lionel's niece (daughter of René, Lionel's older brother) through WhatsApp, on June 30, 2021, who responded, "It gives me great pleasure that you reached out to me, and I would like very much to know you. This is a difficult time; the corona virus is making us crazy. But hopefully we will have the opportunity to share. I believe we both have a lot of wonderful things to communicate to each other. Lionel, your and Barbara's father, was not only my uncle but my godfather and idol! I met him when he was able to return to France after World War II."

Micheline would later email:

>My father René's family (Louis and Madeleine, Andrée and Lionel Durand) traveled to New York by ship in 1942. Louis Durand, who was a career diplomat, was ambassador pro tempore in Paris between 1939 and 1941. All the family visited us in Saint-Germain-sur Morin before they left for NEW YORK CITY; they stayed with us for a few weeks before going to the States and Haïti. When Louis Durand, our grandfather died, he was living in Port-au-Prince with his wife, daughter, and son-in-law. Our grandmother, Maman Madeleine, came to France and lived near our house in Saint-Germain-sur-Morin in a small apartment rented by Lionel.
>
>Lionel was buried in Saint-Germain-sur-Morin, in the place bought by my father René for him and our mother, and your sister Barbara is now in the same grave, not very far from our grandmother Madeleine's.

Micheline Durand introduced Morgan to her older brother, Michel, who was kind enough to email him about Lionel, his and Micheline's uncle. Michelin wrote, "My brother is the one who knows Lionel and that time better than anyone. He will be happy to email you."

Michel playing Count Basie

The following are italicized highlights of Michel Durand's July 25, 2023, email, followed by Morgan's short response.

> *Our father,* René, decided *to stay in France during the war; he was married. I was born in 1938. We heard about the whole family (Louis, Madeleine,* Andrée, and Lionel) *throughout the war, as they did send us many packs of clothes and food. Every Christmas, we received a giant box... It was a big turkey! We had food for a full week.*
>
> *As far I can remember, it was in 1943, we had a message in the box of food or clothes, written by Lionel, telling us that he was a reporter working in New York under the name of Jean Clover, and that we could hear him on a French radio station which was relaying news from the US about France. Otherwise, it*

was very hard to exchange information between the US and Europe. Finally, we heard Lionel on Voice of America radio saying hello to us, his beloved French family, during one of his reports.

Finally, the D Day Invasion in Normandy came on June 6, 1944, and by July 1944, the US army was close to Paris. About 30 US military trucks were parked in front of our house in Saint Germain sur Morin, and I went (I was 7) with my father René and welcomed the US soldiers. They offered to send a letter to Lionel through their own military mail system. This was the start of direct communication with the US family. My father's father was dead, but his mother was still alive, living in New York (or Port-au-Prince, I don't know).

While Lionel frequently came to France after the war as part of his work, he ultimately came here to live when he began working at Newsweek *in 1956. I can remember his office, on Champs Elysées in Paris, as he invited me sometimes to have a look at his work. I was eighteen, and I was, of course, very impressed! When Lionel first came to live and work in Paris in 1956, he initially rented a small apartment near us in Saint Germain sur Morin.*

Lionel would often come over on summer Sundays to have lunch with us, and, as he was working so hard during the week, I

*remember those Sunday lunches always
ended with a significant sleeping period
for him.*

*As the small village of Saint Germain sur Morin was
about 30 miles away from Paris, I had to take two
trains every day to go to my high school, spending
three hours per day, and waking up very early in the
morning. Lionel generously helped pay for my school
tuition. When Lionel moved to Paris in 1957, he invited
me to live with him and his family in Paris. He was
traveling most of the time, and I was often with Irène
(your sister Barbara's mother) more than with Lionel.*

*But at least during weekends, Lionel was there, and I
learned that he was a very good guitar player, and he
had plenty of jazz records (Benny Goodman (1909-
1986), Count Basie (1904-1984), Duke Ellington
(1899-1974), and so on!*

Morgan responded, "Hi, Michel. So grateful and
honored to connect with you, your son Olivier and your sister
Micheline. Lionel loved jazz, and I wonder if that correlates
in a small way to his sensational career as a writer. When I see
the photo of Lionel's fingers rhythmically crafting stories
from his typewriter, it suggests that writing for him was like
playing the jazz that he loved: spontaneity, concentration,
experimentation, and playing off the cultural and political
buzz in the streets. I suspect that Lionel may have, at times,
improvised when developing reports or interviewing the likes
of Khrushchev, Picasso, de Gaulle, Hilda Doolittle, and the
Swedish heavyweight boxing champion, Ingemar Johanson."

Barbara and Irène

Lionel, Jérémy, Noémie, Lionel's daughter, and
Alessia, Jérémy's baby, 2015

Jérémy's wife Chiara and two daughters, Alessia and Elisa, 2023

Barbara and Jérémy, 2008

Lionel's wife and daughter: Aurélie and Charlie,
and Lionel, 2023

****

Lionel Changeur sat for extended interviews with the authors, about Lionel Durand, Barbara, and Irène.

We were curious, for example, to know in what religion Lionel and Jérémy had been raised. According to the Jewish tradition of Irène's family, her daughter Barbara and Barbara's children would be considered Jewish in the Jewish Faith Tradition. Lionel reported that he only learned that his grandmother Irène was Jewish when he was fifteen years old.

It was and remains a sensitive subject for Morgan's nephews, and one which is only just beginning to be fully understood. Having spent extensive time researching Irène's family, the authors shared what they had uncovered in several books and other documents which described Irene's family life before WWII, as well as their escape from the Nazis and finding safe refuge and starting a new life in the USA. Leaving from Lisbon, Portugal, Irène arrived in Baltimore, Maryland, in July of 1942. She was seventeen. On the passenger manifest, she was clearly identified as being Hebrew.

****

Irène's first cousin, Victor Brombert

One of Irène's first cousins, Victor Brombert, became a highly decorated US soldier who returned to Europe to fight for their adopted homeland and for the relatives that they had left behind. Victor fought on the beaches of Normandy and in the Battle of the Bulge. The autobiography he wrote late in life is called *"Trains of Thought: From Paris to Omaha Beach, Memories of a Wartime Youth."* He was part of the elite intelligence unit of primarily Jewish immigrants known as 'the Ritchie Boys' (Camp Ritchie, Maryland). Because they knew the German language, culture, and New York City psychology, they were assigned to every major combat unit in Europe to interrogate German prisoners of war and gather key tactical intelligence on Nazi troop movements, strength, and positions. Their important work was recognized and honored for helping save countless lives of Americans and their Allies. Victor discovered that their aunt Anya, who had gone missing in a roundup of foreign Jews in Nice, had died in Auschwitz.

We do not know how Irène incorporated her Jewish identity into her life over the years other than to note that she apparently lived openly as a Jew when married to Lionel. Lionel's *Newsweek* boss, Ben Bradlee mentions Irène in his autobiography, *"A Good Life: Newspapering and Other Adventures,"* and affectionately described her as "Toto, a Jew from Brooklyn." So, before she lost Lionel, Irène may have felt safe enough and secure enough to live openly as a Jew. Perhaps that sense of security all changed for her when Lionel died, and she suddenly had to raise their eight-year-old Barbara alone. One can only wonder why Irène was reluctant to share her Jewish heritage until later in life, and why she did not share it with Lionel and Jérémy when they were young boys.

Morgan's nephew, Lionel Changeur, filled in some of the blanks: "When I was a child, I called Grandma Irène "Ninamama" and that's how we call her to this day. Ninamama (Nina) kept a lot of matters secret. Since the family of my father (François Changeur) was Catholic, we were raised Catholic. My mother Barbara was not fascinated by religion. Grandma Irène spent a lot of time with me when I was a child. She was fluent in English and in German. My mother had a bachelor's degree in German, and she worked as an intern in the *Nouvel Observateur* (prominent weekly French magazine) founded by Jean Daniel, who knew Lionel Durand. But my mother never became a journalist as she wanted at age nineteen to take care of her new baby. She stopped studying. My grandma was furious about this. She wanted a brighter future for Barbara, to become a famous TV journalist. She wanted her to be like Anne Sinclair, US born in 1948, who hosted one of the most popular political shows for more than 13 years on TFI, a European TV channel. I was baptized and attended catechism classes. But I was a rebel. Perhaps I knew that something was wrong. Ninamama told me that she was Jewish when I was around 15 and somewhat uneducated. I did not know the real meaning of being Jewish. Then Grandma started to be somewhat more open about her race and explained some Judaic rites with salt, but she never avoided foods such as pork. She explained that she had to hide her Jewish identity, to get rid of her accent. I was, I could say, her confidant."

Newlyweds, Lionel and Irène

"I remember being told that my grandfather, Lionel Durand, asked Irène after meeting her, 'Are you already engaged?' She said yes, and Lionel said. 'Well, tell him *I'm going to marry you.*'"

"At that time living in New York City, Irène could not take the bus with Lionel or eat in the same restaurant. Grandma suffered a lot from this segregation and discrimination. When Barack Obama was elected President, it was one of her most beautiful days! The day of revenge! She never mentioned her cousins by name. Fifteen or eighteen years ago, she received a phone call from a German attorney who oversaw reparations paid for the Holocaust. The attorney mentioned one cousin (a woman) who had to share an amount of the reparation. When the check arrived, Ninamama said, 'What was all the fuss about? It was by no means a ridiculous amount of money!'"

"At the age of 96, after suffering Covid-19, Nina is very fragile and silent. Fortunately, she is at peace, and I can see in her eyes that she asks herself, 'What am I doing in this world?' The Rothschild Foundation was her retirement home in Paris. That is an ironic coincidence for she basically had little consideration for Jewish traditions. But was she missing the chance to assimilate Jewish wisdom? In July 2020, we moved Grandmother next to Belgium, in the North of France, because the Rothschild Foundation retirement home in Paris was very disappointing."

Irène passed away on June 9, 2022, reunited with her beloved Lionel.

****

We suspect that one of the reasons Irène and Lionel settled in France was that they would have encountered less prejudice there than in the US. From many accounts, including Lionel's, France was a more tolerant and welcoming place for them to live and to raise Barbara.

Barbara and Lionel, courtesy of Jérémy Changeur

"As soon as I saw you, I knew a grand adventure was going to happen." Winnie the Pooh

Smiling Lionel Durand

Appendix 1

French Resistance Medal

Vivre libre ou mourir
(Live free or die)
Motto of the French Resistance

Photo of Morgan holding the Resistance Medal

In recognition of, and to honor Lionel's war service in the French Resistance under the Nazi Occupation, an authentic Resistance medal hangs on Morgan's wall. We view the medal with reverence and pride. The Resistance medal is the actual decoration bestowed by the French Committee of National Liberation based in the United Kingdom during World War II. It was established by a decree of General Charles de Gaulle on February 9, 1943, to recognize the remarkable acts of faith and courage that, in France, in the empire and abroad, have contributed to the resistance of the French people against the enemy and against its accomplices since June 18, 1940.

The Resistance medal is a 37 mm in diameter circular medal struck from bronze. Its slightly concave obverse displays at center its principal design, a vertical Cross of Lorraine with the relief semicircular inscription of the date of General de Gaulle's appeal of June 18, 1940, "XVIII.VI. MCMXL" (18.06.1940) bisected by the lower part of the cross. The reverse bears the relief image of an unfurling ribbon with the relief inscription in Latin, "PATRIA NON IMMEMOR, *THE NATION DOES NOT FORGET*"

The suspension is cast as an integral part of the medal. The Resistance medal hangs from a 36 mm wide black silk moiré (wavy texture) ribbon with six vertical red stripes of varying widths, 3 mm wide edge stripes, two 1 mm wide central stripes 2 mm apart, and two 1 mm wide stripes 6 mm from the central stripes.

The Resistance medal was awarded to approximately 38,288 living persons and 24,463 posthumously.

Appendix 2

George Polk Memorial Award 1960

Lionel Durand

Osborn Elliott (1924-2008), editor of *Newsweek* magazine for sixteen years, accepted the Polk Award for Lionel in New York City. In Paris, the Anglo-American Press Association of Paris (AAPA) along with *Newsweek*, arranged Lionel's memorial service. The US Ambassador to France eulogizing Lionel in Paris was Amory Houghton (1899-1981) whose first cousin was Katherine Hepburn's mother.

After the war, Lionel worked for the *Paris Presse* as New York and UN Bureau Chief before returning to France as its foreign editor. In 1956 he joined *Newsweek* as a staff correspondent in Paris and became *Newsweek's* Paris Bureau Chief in 1958.

Thanks to the 1950's Overseas Press Club *Bulletins* in the archives, we were able to track his journalistic career progression; his various promotions, reporting assignments, exclusive interviews, election to the Executive Committee of the Anglo-American Press Association of Paris, chairing their Dinner Committee for the annual back-tie dinner and even a 1958 ski vacation in the French Alps were all dutifully noted and recorded in the weekly *Bulletin*.

And then, in January of 1961, the *Bulletin* sadly reported news of his tragic death - dying in his sleep - just weeks after turning 40. He had been interviewing Muslim leaders and was covering the violence and unrest that had erupted at the Casbah in Algiers when a tear-gas canister landed at his feet. Choking and gasping for air, he nevertheless, managed to make it out of the melee and successfully filed his story.

The George Polk Award, given by The Overseas Press Club of America which is the nation's oldest and largest association of journalists engaged in international news. Every April, it awards the most prestigious prizes devoted exclusively to international news coverage. It was founded in 1939 by nine foreign correspondents in New York City, and has grown worldwide to nearly five hundred members, all media industry leaders. The club seeks to maintain an international association of journalists working in the US and abroad to encourage the highest standards of professional integrity and skill in the reporting of news and to work toward better communication and understanding among people. The club's mission is to foster excellence in news reporting, advance press freedom, and promote good fellowship among colleagues while educating a new generation of journalists.

In its story about the Award, the Overseas Press Corp 1961 dateline carried a photo of reporter Lionel Durand in a press conference towering over Nikita Khrushchev. (See page 107)

In June 1961 the *Bulletin* announced that, in a formal ceremony on the 17th anniversary of D-Day, Lionel's name had been added to the OPC Memorial Room Honor Roll. The story explained: "This roster, which honors newsmen killed in the performance of their journalistic duties, now totals 93 names." (The photo below that accompanies the story shows his name prominently displayed on the Honor Roll wall in the right-hand column at the top.)

TAPS FOR HONORED NEWSMEN (l. to r.) Bugler Fred Bechtel; Club President Dick Johnston; Major Louis Barish; Commander Oliver Jones; Mrs. Chester Kronfeld; Ben Wright; Captain Patrick Garzione; and Burnet Hershey. Plaques were unveiled at Memorial Room ceremony, June 6.

Excerpt from the 1961 Dateline for: The George Polk Memorial Award 1960 (presented posthumously)

> AWARD: Lionel Durand, Newsweek's Paris bureau chief, died Jan. 14, 1961, in Paris of a heart attack. It was a result of his being tear-gassed in Algeria, while covering riots that had erupted in the Casbah. He'd gone there to interview Moslem leaders. Among his last stories were "Algeria - You-You-You-You" and "Into the Eye of the Storm." He died quietly in his sleep of a heart attack.

So ended "Epitaph—A Reporter," *Newsweek's* account of Lionel Durand's death:

> *Durand, who for two years was Newsweek's Paris bureau chief, had lived life to the hilt. His interests were legion, so were his talents. Counting Picasso among his intimate friends, he was himself a painter of quality, a nimble guitarist, and fluent in six languages.*

178

He could cover a Khrushchev press conference one day and a bullfight in Spain the next.

But the big story for Durand was always politics. One of the first to predict de Gaulle's return to power, Durand was still covering a part of the de Gaulle story when he went to Africa to cover the Algerian war. He visited the Casbah to interview Moslem leaders during one of the riots and was caught in a crossfire as police tried to quell the disturbance. Though a tear-gas bomb exploded at his feet he went, coughing and sputtering, half-walking, half-running, to file his story from a cable office miles away. He returned to the Paris bureau exhausted, the tear gas having added to the strain of the previous months. Then, Friday night, January 13, his last story written and dispatched, Lionel Durand went quietly to sleep.

Lionel Durand in deep thought

OPC Digital Archives Help Uncover Lost Family History

Posted July 11, 2023, by Overseas Press Club of America

Dear Editor of the Overseas Press Club Bulletin,

In the eleven short months since 1,751 historical OPC Bulletins and other unique OPC records have been digitalized and preserved online at Archive.org, they have been accessed by 5,909 unique individuals. As one of those individuals, I would like to briefly share with you my personal story of accessing them, what I learned, and to express my most sincere and heartfelt gratitude.

I was born in 1944 and will turn 79 in just a few months. Until only recently, I have never known who my father was. As a young child, my mother had relinquished me, putting me up for adoption, and declaring to the court that my unnamed father was dead. The unstated implication was that he had been killed in World War II. This, it would turn out, was a lie.

I have always yearned to know who my father was. With the dogged assistance of my beloved friend and a professional Investigative Genetic Genealogist, John F. Suggs, the two of us ultimately discovered through DNA analysis that my father was, in fact, Lionel Durand, a highly respected and accomplished journalist and a member of the OPC of America and the Anglo-American Press Association of Paris.

Born in Haiti in 1920, the son of the last prewar Haitian Ambassador to France, Lionel studied at the Sorbonne, Heidelberg and Oxford and spoke French, English, German, Russian, Spanish and Italian. He and his family would find themselves trapped in France when the Germans invaded in 1940. The *New York Times*, along with the *Bulletin*, recounted that Lionel had fought in the French Resistance and was "twice arrested by the Gestapo and twice escaped."

In the US National Archives, we discovered as part of a wartime special investigation by the FBI, a report, filed under the signature of J. Edgar Hoover, that noted that Lionel's father, Louis Durand, had returned to his home in Le Havre, France on July 16, 1941, and encountered four German soldiers who demanded his passports and those of his family. The soldiers confiscated the following: "diplomatic passports and passports of Durand's family; exequatur and act of nomination by Haitian Government; marriage certificate of Durand's son, Lionel; official and private letters; all consular seals; blank passports; and notes belonging to Durand's son and a photograph. They were now without any diplomatic identification papers to protect them in occupied France.

In the summer of 1942, the family finally successfully fled France for New York, where Lionel was appointed director of Voice of America's French section regularly broadcasting to the people of occupied France. It was while there, at the Voice of America desk in New York, that he met my mother who was working down the hall at the Office of

War Information department. Besides the racial challenges stemming from the fact that Lionel was Black, and my mother was White, there was also an additional complication due to the fact that my mother was married at the time to a soldier serving overseas. Thus, my very "being" represented a scandal for her that she ultimately resolved by unilaterally declaring my father dead and turning me over for adoption.

After the war, from 1945-1948, Lionel would work for the *Paris Presse* as New York and UN bureau chief before returning to France as its foreign editor. In 1956 he joined *Newsweek* as a staff correspondent in Paris and became *Newsweek's* Paris bureau chief in 1958. Thanks to the 1950's *Bulletins* in the archives, I was able to track his journalistic career progression. His various promotions, reporting assignments, exclusive interviews, election to the Executive Committee of the Anglo-American Press Association of Paris, chairing their Dinner Committee for the annual black-tie dinner and even a 1958 ski vacation in the French Alps were all dutifully noted and recorded in the weekly *Bulletin*.

And then, in January of 1961, the *Bulletin* sadly reported news of his tragic death just weeks after turning 40. He had been interviewing Muslim leaders and was covering the violence and unrest that had erupted at the Casbah in Algiers when a tear gas canister landed at his feet. Choking and gasping for air, he nevertheless managed to make it out of the melee and successfully filed his story. Tragically, he never recovered from his injuries and, shortly thereafter, died of a heart attack in his sleep.

The *Bulletin* would continue to report on him in the coming weeks. First, to announce the naming of his successor,

Larry Collins, as *Newsweek's* Paris Bureau Chief and then to announce that the OPC had voted to posthumously award both him and Henry N. Taylor of Scripps-Howard Newspapers, the 1961 George Polk Memorial Award "For best reporting, requiring exceptional courage and enterprise abroad." (Note: The final George Polk Memorial Award was bestowed in 1973.)

In its story about the award, the OPC's 1961 annual Dateline carried a photo of him towering over Nikita Khrushchev in an informal press gaggle. (I had never seen this picture before, and it simply took my breath away. Thank you OPC for making this photo available to me!) Finally, in June, the *Bulletin* announced that, in a formal ceremony on the 17th anniversary of D-Day, his name had been added to the OPC Memorial Room Honor Roll. The story explained that "This roster, which honors newsmen killed in the performance of their journalistic duties, now totals 93 names." (A photo that accompanies the story shows his name prominently displayed on the Honor Roll wall. Seeing the photo of Lionel's name for the very first time brought me to tears.)

I want to close by thanking everyone in your organization who made the effort required for digitizing all the OPC historical Bulletins and records and thereby making these archives available online to the public and to me. Specifically, I want to thank by name, Patricia Kranz, your executive director, who so kindly reached out to inform us of the existence of these treasures. Patricia, you have given an old man a truly priceless gift - my father!

Cordially,

Morgan Zo Callahan

Appendix 3

The *New York Times*
January 15, 1961, Obituary

Lionel Durand, A Newsman, Dies

Paris, Jan. 14 - Lionel Durand, Paris correspondent of *Newsweek* magazine, died today at the age of 39. On Friday he told friends he had inhaled tear gas during the recent disturbance in Algiers, which he covered for his magazine. He said he experienced difficulty catching his breath.

Born in Haiti, M. Durand spent most of his youth and received all of his education in France.

After the fall of France, he joined the French Resistance and was twice arrested by the Gestapo and twice escaped. In 1943 he made his way to the United States, where he became director of the French section of the Voice of America.

When France was liberated, M. Durand returned to Paris to become foreign editor of the afternoon daily, *Paris-Presse*. He served for several years as that paper's correspondent in New York.

He returned to Paris in 1956 for *Newsweek*. It was during the four years that followed that he established his reputation as a correspondent who understood both the people he was reporting on and the people—the American people—he was reporting to.

As a former member of the Resistance, he knew most of the major figures of that heroic era up to and including President de Gaulle. As he was also the intimate of art figures, including Pablo Picasso, and of the directors of the Paris Opera, M. Durand wrote magazine articles for many American publications on the Paris art, music and cultural scenes.

He leaves his wife and daughter.

Appendix 4

Tampa Bay Times St. Petersburg, Jan 15, 1961, Obituary
Lionel Durand Dies, Magazine Bureau Chief

NEW YORK (UPI): Lionel Durand, 39, chief of the Paris bureau of *Newsweek* magazine, died early yesterday at his home in the French capital, the magazine announced last night.

Durand, who had been suffering from the effects of tear gas inhaled when covering the Algerian riots early last month, had been planning to enter a hospital for a rest. His associates said the doctor believed death was due to a heart attack.

Born in Port-au-Prince, Haiti, he was educated at the Sorbonne, Heidelberg University and Oxford University. His father was Haitian minister to France prior to World War II.

During the war, Durand served with the French Resistance Movement and twice escaped after being captured by the Nazis.

He is survived by his wife, Irène, and a daughter, Barbara Eve Sophie, 8 years old.

Appendix 5

Newsweek January 23, 1961, Obituary

Irène with admiring eyes for Lionel

Epitaph - A Reporter

> Durand Paris
> Proceed Algeria
> Cover Violence
> For Friday File

Between this curt instruction and the thousand-word cable that reached *Newsweek's* New York office a month ago, there was a time of tear gas and rioting, and the agony of Frenchmen shooting Frenchmen. The settlers of Algiers had gone out into the street to protest President de Gaulle's decision to let Algeria decide its own future; the Moslems of Algeria had poured forth from the Casbah to cheer for independence. The gendarmes fired on both, and in the no man's land between rioters and police a tear-gas shell burst at the feet of a tall, US newsman. That man was Lionel Durand, 39, Newsweek's Paris bureau chief, doing his job - as he always did - in the thick of the news.

Coughing and sputtering, Durand carried on, taking notes. Afterward, he half-walked, half ran to a cable office several miles away. His report told how he had gone into the hate-laden Casbah to interview Moslem leaders. He did not mention the damage to his lungs.

Modest Man: That, of course, was typical of correspondent Durand. For Durand was a modest man - with nothing to be modest about. Born in Port-au-Prince, the son of a prewar Haitian Ambassador to France, he worked all over the world - in the US, where he headed the French section of the "Voice of America"; in the Middle East, and Africa; in Moscow, where in 1957 he was one of the first Western newsmen to talk to Nikita S. Khrushchev. During World War II, he fought in the Resistance.

Of all the big news figures he knew, perhaps the closest to him was his painter friend Pablo Picasso. When *Newsweek* printed a picture story on Picasso's exhibition in London, the great artist supplied his own captions to go with Durand's photographs (*Newsweek*, July 4, 1960). "I did this," explained Picasso "out of friendship for Lionel."

Durand's range and depth amazed his colleagues. He was a painter of quality, he played a wicked guitar, he had studied at the Sorbonne, Heidelberg, and Oxford, he spoke Russian, German, Spanish, and Italian as well as French and English. One day, he flew to Spain for a bullfighting story; the next, to Geneva to interview heavyweight champ, Ingemar Johanson. His interests were legion and so were his talents.

> *Yet the big story for Durand was always politics. In 1957, while Charles de Gaulle was cloistered in his rural farmhouse, out of power, it seemed for good, Durand was one of the first to report that de Gaulle would be back. Others threw doubt on his stories, but history proved Durand right.*

Still covering the de Gaulle story, Durand bid *au revoir* to his wife, Irène, and 8-year-old daughter, Barbara, and set out last month on his last big assignment—the rioting in Algiers. He returned to the Paris bureau exhausted, the tear gas having added to the strain he had been feeling during recent months. Last week, he contributed to three stories that appear in this week's issue: On NATO (page 26), Belgium (page 40), and The Periscope (page 10). Then, on Friday night, his last story written and dispatched, Durand went to bed for the last time. He died quietly in his sleep of a heart attack.

JANUARY 23, 1961 25c
[INDEX—PAGE ?]

'New Frontier'—Special Section

Lionel Durand's January 23, 1961, Obituary appears in this issue of *Newsweek:*

> *To all the men and women of Newsweek, and to the mountain climbers and statesmen, the actors, artists, writers, teachers, singers, diplomats, and elevator operators who counted themselves his friends, Durand was more than a first-class reporter. He was kindness, resourcefulness, generosity, humor, and courage - and those are the qualities for which he will be missed.*

Appendix 6

Haitian Journalist Has Died in Love with Spain, 1961

A HAITIAN JOURNALIST HAS DIED IN LOVE WITH SPAIN

LIONEL DURAND HAS BEEN INDIRECTLY A VICTIM OF DECEMBER 1960 EVENTS IN ALGIERS.

FROM PARIS, (CHONICA RADIOTELEGRAFICA OF OUR CORRESPONDENT)

Today we have buried in a locality very close to Paris Lionel Durand, correspondent for all of Europe, writing for the American weekly *Newsweek*, who died at the age of thirty-nine of a heart failure caused in large part by the tear gas inflicted on his somewhat threatened constitution. Durand suffered the effects of the explosion of a grenade and other violent incidents that he had to endure in Algiers that occurred on December 10th.

Lionel Durand - of dark color and the son of an ambassador in Paris of his country Haiti - was a very accomplished product of American and French journalism. Haiti is a curious enclave where people meet and complement each other in French and North American culture. When I was there, I was surprised like any traveler to find one of the most select and refined minorities in the Caribbean...They are multiglot and members of intellectual groups that alternate their studies in Paris and at the "Colored" Universities of the United States. I met Lionel Durand in Paris at the end of the world war and then at the U.N. of New York where he represented the newspaper,

Paris Presse. In 1956, he took on a new role: correspondent, writing in English, for *Newsweek* of New York in Paris. Covering almost the entire European continent, Lionel Durand went quickly anywhere and lit the blaze on current news stories. Durand and I came together many times and always for my benefit. Among so many countries that he knew and visited, one of them constituted his land of predilection, almost of promise: Spain. For our country of Spain was above all the destination of Durand's vacations. In summer and whenever he felt fatigued, he had Spain as his goal. Madrid, Barcelona, Malaga or the Costa Brava? He didn't care which as all was according to the season. For him, summer was synonymous with S'Agaró.

It is possible that we will exceed four million visitors in Spain. Among so many, one, Lionel Durand, will have to be subtracted, only one. But one that has earned us many thousands.

Carlos SENTIS

Appendix 7

Haitian Times August 16, 2019

"First Person" article, "A Father and Son Reunion"

Morgan as a Boy

The Haitian Times, founded in 1999 as a weekly English language digital newspaper, is based in Brooklyn, NY. The newspaper is widely regarded as the most authoritative voice for the Haitian Diaspora. On August 16, 2019, one of the authors, Morgan Zo Callahan, published this personal essay in *The Haitian Times*.

FIRST PERSON - A Father and Son Reunion

I had no idea who my father was for the first 74 years of my life. Given up for adoption, all I knew was what the adoption records stated: that my father had died before I was born. I often wondered who he was. How did he die? Had he even known he was going to be a father?

Since I was born in 1944, was he a soldier? Did he die in the war? Was his death the reason I was put up for adoption? My adoption papers, offering no clues, merely stated about me, Morgan Zo Callahan as a child: "The boy is a dark-complexioned child, thin and wiry with curly brown hair and large somewhat solemn eyes. On . . . the day before his third birthday, the child . . . was brought to the house of adoptive parents. Nothing is known of this child's life up to this date."

I discovered when I was in high school some information about my biological mother. But now as an old man, I was seeking to find the answers about my father that have eluded me all my life, so I submitted my DNA to Ancestry.com. When the results came back, I got my first clue: the DNA showed that my father was of African heritage and that my paternal DNA matches in the database were all Haitians! Unfortunately, because so few Haitians have submitted their DNA for testing, the matches I had were few and only distantly related. So, I hired a professional genetic genealogist, John F. Suggs, to help me in my search.

It was from John that I finally learned who my father was: Lionel Durand, an eminent Haitian journalist. Sadly, I also learned that my father had been alive and well for the first 17 years of my life but had never known of my existence. Lionel Durand had been denied his right to know me—and I him— and to be named as my father on my birth and adoption documents. So, who was my father? I learned that Lionel studied at the Sorbonne, Heidelberg, and Oxford, and spoke French, English, German, Russian, Spanish, and Italian. Lionel's father, Louis Durand (born 1863), was the prewar Haitian ambassador to France.

The Durand family found themselves trapped in France when the Germans invaded in 1940. The *New York Times* recounted that Lionel Durand was a former member of the French Resistance who was "twice arrested by the Gestapo and twice escaped." Lionel faced added difficulties for Blacks fighting in the French Resistance. Former resistance fighter, Philippe de Vomécourt wrote in 1961: "For colored men in France, a 'safe house' or false identity papers were an impossibility. To be a colored man in a district occupied by the Germans was to know that death was near. The Germans had a pathological fear and hatred of colored men."

Yet, in spite of this, Lionel joined and fought in the Resistance. As part of a wartime special investigation by the FBI, a report, filed under the signature of J. Edgar Hoover, noted that Louis Durand, the Haitian Consul in Le Havre France, had returned to his home on July 16, 1941, and encountered four German soldiers who demanded his passports and those of his family.

The soldiers confiscated the following: diplomatic passports and passports of Durand's family; exequatur and act of nomination by Haitian Government; marriage certificate of Durand's son, Lionel; official and private letters; all consular seals; blank passports; and notes belonging to Durand's son and a photograph. They were now without any identification papers to protect them in occupied France. In the summer of 1942, the family finally successfully fled France for NEW YORK CITY, where Lionel was appointed director of Voice of America's French section regularly broadcasting to the peoples of occupied France.

****

He knew Paris as well as he knew the keyboard of his battered typewriter, and there was never an American visitor who wanted a glass of wine, or a wise briefing on French politics, or a gay laugh in a bistro, who did not get it freely from him. This was Lionel Durand.
Haiti Sun, January 29, 1961

Lionel returned to France in 1956 and eventually joined *Newsweek*. "As a former member of the Resistance he knew most of the major figures of that heroic era up to and including President de Gaulle." Lionel, a painter himself, must have been so energized being friends with Pablo Picasso. When Newsweek did a picture story on Picasso's London exhibition, Pablo supplied his own captions for Lionel's photographs. "I did this," explained Picasso, "out of friendship for Lionel."

In 1957, Durand was among the first reporters from the West to talk to Nikita S. Khrushchev. Lionel was covering the four-day and four-night celebration of Bolshevism's 40th anniversary. Long-winded NSK got things rolling with a three-hour speech to 17,000 Communists from 61 nations. "His sputniks launched and his rule secure, Nikita S. Khrushchev was rattling rockets, and talking peace on Soviet terms."

After a January 8, 1961, referendum on Algerian self-determination, Charles de Gaulle declared the results of 16.9 million votes "to be striking." 72% of French citizens of France and Algeria approved de Gaulle's plan to end the Algerian War of Independence (1954-1962). The settlers of Algiers went into the streets to protest while the Muslims cheered for independence. The police fired on both continents. 1.5 million died in the war say Algerian historians while their French counterparts say four hundred thousand from both sides died, horrific numbers. Covering Algiers cost Lionel his life. Lionel died from a heart attack on January 14, 1961, a result of being tear gassed in Algeria.

Lionel Durand was survived by his Jewish-German wife, Irène Lipsz of New York City, born in Leipzig,1924. Escaping from the Nazis, Irène arrived in Baltimore, July 1942; she married Lionel in 1948. Their daughter, Barbara, was born July 16, 1952, in Neuilly, France. Sadly, Barbara died in Hôpital de la Salpêtrière, Paris. Lionel, his wife and daughter, all died without ever knowing about me - his son. My new-found father, Lionel Durand, has been an enrichment of my life, already happy with cherished family and friends.

Discovering Lionel is being reborn in my father's DNA, connecting to Haiti and Africa. I have been blessed to meet

Haitian born cousins, feelings of pride in my Haitian blood and in the life of a remarkable Haitian reporter and war hero.

Appendix 8

Conversation with Dr. François Pierre-Louis Jr.

> *"Never give up on hope. Most of the greatest achievements of humanity were accomplished by tired, discouraged people who never gave up on hope. Anything is possible . . . if you truly believe."*
> Timothy Pina, Hearts for Haiti: Book of Poetry & Inspiration

> *"Life can only be understood backwards, but it must be lived forwards."* Søren Kierkegaard

At an early December 2020 Zoom meeting of Faith in Action International (directed by my long-time friend John Baumann SJ) in a breakout room for Haiti, I met the distinguished Dr. François Pierre-Louis Jr. who is a professor of political science at Queens College, City University of New York.

I decided to reach out to him for an interview about his organization in Haiti. He graciously responded, "If it is Father John Baumann that sends you my way, you know the answer will always be yes." François has published several articles in Haitian and Caribbean journals. François' research interests include immigration, transnationalism, and Haitian politics. He has experience as a community organizer in Haiti and the USA, served in the private cabinet of President Jean Bertrand

Aristide in 1991, and as an advisor to Prime Minister Jacques-Édouard Alexis in 2007–2008.

He speaks sagaciously based on his heart-breaking, as well as uplifting, experience, sharpened by scholarly study. We do well to listen.

Dr. Pierre-Louis, 60, grew up in Haiti until 14 years of age, and then in Queens, New York. Haiti has suffered through dictators and contested elections for decades. He lamented that François Duvalier horrifically killed all four of his mother's brothers and many of his male cousins because one of his uncles had openly opposed the dictator and his cruel regime.

He is the author of *"Haitians in New York City: Transnationalism and Hometown Associations."* His articles have appeared in *"US Catholics, Wadabagei, Journal of Haitian Studies, Education and Urban Society,* and *Journal of Black Studies."* Prof. Pierre-Louis coordinated the Chancellor Initiative to help rebuild higher education in Haiti after the 2010 earthquake. He was able to extend higher education to locations outside of Port-au-Prince.

On a September 28, 2015, YouTube video on GCTV with Bill Miller, Dr. François talks about Haiti and the tragic consequences of its January 12, 2010, 7.8 earthquake when 85% of Port-au-Prince's buildings were destroyed. François, who was in Haiti at the time, talked about the feeling of powerlessness ("a horrible memory") as well as noting the resiliency of the people to help each other out despite a lack of resources. Many citizens, including François, distributed food and water. Dr. François talked about hopes for governing Haiti as a democracy, with a decentralization where the people can use financial aid in their own communities. So much of the aid to Haiti is given to experts who devise plans which are never carried out due to a lack of infrastructure and government corruption. Some from the Haitian Diaspora, independent of the state, are raising money and returning to their hometowns to organize and provide resources such as hunger relief and education.

****

On January 5, 2021, I conversed by telephone with François, who was cordial and generous with his time.

MZC: Hello, François. So appreciative you would take the time to speak about Haiti, your life, and your work with our mutual friend, John Baumann, through Faith in Action International Haiti. How are you doing? Are you still teaching?

FP-L: It is a pleasure talking with you. I read your fascinating *Haitian Times article* about the remarkable father you discovered: Haitian Lionel Durand.

I hope you are doing all right in Los Angeles where we see COVID-19 is raging. We have had a tough time in my family. I lost my mother to COVID-19 in May 2020, and my brother was six months in a coma. So, I know the virus is no joke. Life goes on. I continue teaching college online using Blackboard.

MZC: I am so sorry for your great loss, François. May your mother enjoy Eternal Life. Glad your brother was able to survive. Hope you all take good care. Best wishes and blessings.

What was your childhood like and how was it that you came to live in New York City?

FP-L: Thanks. You as well. Let me tell you about my early years. I was born in Cap-Haïtien in 1960. I stayed in Haiti until I was 14, when I joined my family in New York in 1974. Haiti, during my growing-up years, was the best time of my life. I did not suffer from the lack of basic needs. My father first came to NY in 1965. I was living with my mother in Port-au-Prince, later moving to Northeast Haiti. My mother's sister and family lived there. My mother's aunt was associated with a butcher's market, so when it came to food, we never had any issues. I did not see myself as poor. It was really nice growing up in Haiti, a country with beautiful nature, though now it has suffered deterioration with so much deforestation, erosion of soil, lack of infrastructure and leadership, and poverty. It is not as lovely as when I was growing up.

I went to a Christian Brothers school; some classmates were the sons of lawyers, businessmen, and professors. One classmate's father was the commanding officer of the town. I realized there was a privileged class in Haiti. Then I moved back to Cap-Haïtien, and the first year I went to high school, also a school for many privileged children. My godmother's husband was the chief judge in Cap-Haïtien. I had to take a test to get into the school, so I was happy I passed. After my first year, I came to the US.

MZC: Where did you live and go to school in the US? What was your family and school life like?

FP-L: Both my mother and father were already in New York. My dad was living in Brooklyn and from there we came to

Queens. I discovered my dad was divorced from my mother. Two of us lived with Mom, and two of us lived with Dad. We were able to visit each weekend, and I was able to spend time with my mother. After Jamaica High School, I went to college, Queens College.

My dad bought a house in Queens. In high school, I knew there was discrimination, but my teachers welcomed me, were interested in me, and took me on trips such as to Washington, DC: In the summer I read so many good books. I got into Tolstoy, *Anna Karenina* and *War and Peace*. I was 17. A social science teacher gave me the classic political novel, *All the King's Men* by Robert Penn Warren. I got accepted to some colleges, but my father worried that something might happen to me, so he did not want me to go far away. I went to Queens College which had a lot of Haitian students who had a similar history.

MZC: How did you get into politics and organizing? What did you learn as a young man about Haiti, your birthplace?

FP-L: I got to meet many people and started my political education as well. When I lived in Haiti, I did not know the history of my father and mother. No one told us. I learned that all four of my mother's brothers were killed by Duvalier. My mother suffered a lot. I met political exiles from Haiti and started interacting with students from Haiti who were activists. I was encouraged to get involved.

I thought I could someday go back to Haiti to help after Duvalier. My father listened to the Opposition Radio in New York. I started to understand what was happening in Haiti and joined a student group on campus. Eventually I joined a

Haitian political party. I quit school in 1980 and spent more time with Haitian refugees. There was a church where I taught Haitians ESL in the evening. I became more engaged. I started to protest along with several classmates. We met with political leaders who were exiled by Duvalier. My purpose was to help create a more just society in Haiti.

MZC: How did you meet John Baumann?

FP-L: I was organizing in Brooklyn in the 1980s. Herbert White, who was affiliated with Saul Alinsky and John Baumann's organization PICO, gave me my first training in Florida. I left Brooklyn and did organizing in Haiti for six years, from 1986–1991. I was put in jail twice, once for four days, once for two days. I was on the death-squad's hit list. I met Aristide, then Father Aristide, who was a pastor in a slum in Port-au-Prince and very much involved in organizing. I got to know him very well. When he was elected president, I became a member of his private cabinet. The coup took place in 1991, and I moved back to the US in 1992. I reconnected with Herb White and his wife, Jessica, who had organized with Herb in the Philippines. I started a project in Brooklyn with $6,000 that Jessica gave me from her organization.

I met Fr. John in the summer of 1996. I remember we met in Oakland, California, and had coffee. John is such a good man. He came to New York and John said yes, he would collaborate with me. I did some training with PICO. John was so self-effacing; you would never know he was a priest. He doesn't talk too much. But he observes and he acts. He gives all of himself for the good of others. There were people in the network whom I also appreciated and respected such as Jose Carrasco and Ron Snyder, who is with Faith in Action to this day. These people inspired me, and I appreciated their efforts for social justice.

MZC: How did your work with Father John start out?

FP-L: I brought PICO, now named Faith in Action (FIA), to the five boroughs of New York City. In 2001, I left as the full-time director because I decided to take a position as a professor. I stayed on as a consultant in Brooklyn. I kept in contact with John. When John's organization went international in El Salvador and Rwanda, he wanted me to start organizing in Haiti. I knew Haitian politics and the dangers of being in Haiti.

When the earthquake hit Haiti, I was there. I decided to help the colleges reestablish themselves. We were able to get students in rural areas greater access to education. I was spending more time in Haiti and told John I would like to start a project in Haiti. That was 2013; John obviously supported me, and I met with the bishops in Haiti who supported the idea, and we launched our community organization in 2014. John Baumann has been to Haiti and loves the people. He never complains about the hot weather. He never asks for anything. I can't believe this guy!

MZC: Do you travel often to Haiti? How is your organizing work going?

FP-L: I was in Haiti from 2013 to the end of 2015 as a consultant for Faith in Action Haiti and doing some work for the City University of New York (CUNY) Projects in Haiti. When I came back to be a professor, I still would go to Haiti about every two months. I would go there to meet with leaders in towns, with the bishop and priests; we organized. I put together seven money-making cooperatives with the leadership. Despite the difficulties with COVID-19 and the political turmoil since 2018, the people are mostly hanging on.

Sadly, it's impossible to have a fair election in Haiti because of the many gangs, fully armed individuals. People are being held hostage not only in Port-au-Prince but throughout the country. There is great difficulty in getting the people access to pure water and food. There is a food deficit in Haiti. The young people have so much talent, and they want to do something with their lives. But there is no leadership, few opportunities for work. People go to school and learn trades but have nowhere to go to use those skills. Before they might go to other Caribbean countries or the US but now all this is closed. People must go as far away as Chile and Brazil for work, to see if they can survive.

We must change the way things are done in Haiti, create leadership, get rid of governmental corruption. For the most part, young people have no choice but to join the gangs and engage in the drug trade which is a major supplier to the Caribbean and America. Several organizations are doing their best to improve Haiti's culture, education, standard of living, and leadership.

MZC: What gives you your focus and strength?

FP-L: The Haitian people. And people in general. In essence people are good. I have talked about the conditions in Haiti such as the death squads, the earthquake, the lack of necessities. Yet we have survived, and I believe God is looking after us. Also giving me hope are the possibilities I have seen.

There are positive actions. Together in mutual respect, we give the people the chance to meet and share together, to see who they are (as well as to see who we are), to be able to implement the skills and knowledge they have. I have seen transformation in young people who are able to go to school or get a job. A parent who gets work and is then able to send his/her children to school! You do not need much money to do it. You need to tell people the truth and that whatever they want, with support, they can put their mind and heart into it. You do not do it because you want to be famous or take advantage of any situation or person. You do it because you genuinely care for the people. It is amazing to go to Haiti and see the effective leaders who do serve others, and relatively speaking, they have nothing! I think what amazes people when they visit Haiti is that it is not so much about material goals and benefits the people want as much as fostering the relationships they have with people.

The human connection, something we are losing in the US, losing the primary knowledge that we are first and foremost human beings, no matter what, rich or poor. At the end of the day what is the difference between you and another? In the US usually all our material needs, and more are met, but we tend to lose the human touch. In Haiti you can feel the human connection strongly. I honestly do not know how Haitians have the faith to keep going with so many challenges. I ask myself sometimes: "Would I be able to survive living with so many hardships encountered daily in Haiti?" Today so many have no anchor; they do not even know where the food is coming from. Yet most do not steal or kill; they deal with it in a very decent, human way. This faith and love for the people—despite such trials and tribulation—keeps me going as an activist on behalf of my beloved Haiti. Thank you and God bless you for our conversation.

MZC: Thanks to you, François, and blessings for your work and service, with, from and for our Haitian brothers and sisters and your inspiration for all of us.

Made in the USA
Las Vegas, NV
03 December 2024

13285256R10128